SECRET MISSION
TO THE PHILIPPINES

BY WILLIAM WISE

Detective Pinkerton and Mr. Lincoln
The Spy and General Washington
The Story of Mulberry Bend
When the Saboteurs Came

William Wise

SECRET MISSION
TO THE PHILIPPINES

*The Story of "Spyron" and the American-Filipino
Guerrillas of World War II*

E. P. DUTTON & CO., INC.   NEW YORK

To Millicent

The author is very grateful to Commander Parsons for the information he provided during the preparation of this manuscript.

William Wise

CONTENTS

	Foreword	9
1	Young Man in the Islands	11
2	Peace and War	19
3	The Fall of Manila	27
4	The Intelligence File	39
5	After Corregidor	48
6	Nightmare Voyage	56
7	Send Parsons	67
8	The Odyssey Begins	75
9	Mindanao	84
10	Kangleon, Pendatun and Fertig	96
11	A Rude Awakening	106
12	The Start South	115
13	Jungle Flight	122
14	$50,000—Dead or Alive	135
15	Spyron Flourishes	145
16	The End of the Story	152

Maps

Parsons' Escape Route – 1942	26
Philippines	66

FOREWORD

DURING THE SUMMER OF 1942, A VICTORIOUS JAPANESE
army occupied the Philippine Islands. Several months later,
reports of a guerrilla uprising there reached Douglas
MacArthur's Southwest Pacific Headquarters.

Even though he had recently escaped from Japanese
hands, Commander Charles Parsons of the United States
Navy volunteered to return to enemy-held territory, with a
modern "Message to Garcia" for the Philippine people.
Such was the first mission of "Spyron"—an organization
whose very existence was one of the most closely guarded
military secrets of World War II.

1

YOUNG MAN
IN THE ISLANDS

ONE SUNLIT AFTERNOON IN 1921, A SMALL, RUSTY-looking freighter sailed past the fortress of Corregidor, and entered Manila Bay. The ship's arrival meant little to most of the men aboard. Because they had already been to every corner of the tropics, Manila, the capital of the Philippine Islands, was just another port of call to them.

But to the youngest member of the crew, the ship's arrival was a different matter. Ever since he could remember, Charles Parsons had dreamed of coming out to live in the Philippines. Now, after a land and sea journey of almost ten thousand miles from his native Tennessee, he finally had reached the gateway to the Islands.

When the ship docked, he packed his few belongings and

then climbed one of the ladders to the captain's cabin. Inside, he signed a receipt and was paid his wages.

The narrow cabin was stifling. The captain stood up and wiped his forehead. "Let's go on deck for a couple of minutes," he said. He opened the cabin door, and Parsons followed him over to the ship's rail.

"Have you ever been to the Islands before?" the captain asked him.

"No, sir. This is the first time I've been anywhere—except a few miles from Chattanooga."

"How old are you, Chick?"

"Nineteen."

"Got a job lined up?"

"Not yet, Captain."

"I don't suppose you know any Spanish. It's a help out here because a lot of the people around the Islands don't speak much else. But I guess nobody told you that back home?"

Chick Parsons couldn't help grinning. "I've been studying Spanish," he said, "since my second year in high school."

The captain looked surprised. "Figured things out beforehand, did you?"

Parsons nodded. "I tried to—as much as I could."

The captain started to fill the bowl of his pipe. "What sort of job do you figure you'll be looking for?"

"Some kind of stenographic work," Parsons said. "I know shorthand pretty well. Back home last year I worked as a court stenographer. It was part of my plan, Captain. I thought I'd better pick up some practical experience—and a little cash—before I left Tennessee."

The captain struck a match and held it to his pipe. "You're still too bloody young," he muttered between puffs, "to be on your own. All the same, you seem to have a good head on your shoulders. Not like most of the kids who come out here, without the foggiest notion of what they'll be faced with. Half of them can't find proper work, and end up 'on the beach,' scrounging for a few pennies to keep body and soul together."

They stood by the rail for a minute or two, and looked toward the city. "But I don't think that's going to happen to you," the captain finally said. "I've got a hunch you'll land on your feet. In fact, you could wind up making a name for yourself out here in the Islands. I've seen it happen before. Who can say? Fifteen or twenty years from now, they might be talking about Chick Parsons from one end of the Philippines to the other."

The captain put out his hand, wished him good luck, and then turned back to his cabin. Parsons climbed slowly down to the dock.

When he was on land again, he began to smile. Though he was alone in a strange country, possessed very little money, and had neither a job nor even the promise of one, he'd never felt happier in his life. The explanation was simple: He was in the Philippines, the one country in the world where he most wanted to be.

As to the future—and the captain's prophecy—he shrugged. It didn't strike him as likely that in twenty years' time people would be talking about him "from one end of the Philippines to the other." And it certainly never occurred to him that one day, during a bitter war, he might make such a "name" for himself in the Islands that an enemy government would offer a reward for his capture— $50,000, dead or alive.

In Manila, Chick Parsons took a few days off to get his bearings. Then he began to hunt for a job. He didn't accept the first one that came along, though. It would have meant staying in the capital, and at the back of his mind there was the hope that he could find some sort of work that would permit him to travel, not only on Luzon itself but also on some of the other islands, to the south. Just as his few dollars were beginning to run out, he learned of a job that sounded promising.

An official government study of the entire Philippine Territory was about to be undertaken by the Wood-Forbes Investigating Commission. The head of the commission, General Leonard Wood, was in need of a secretary. That afternoon, Chick Parsons appeared at the commission's offices. He said that he knew Spanish, and described his stenographic experience. He was immediately tested on his qualifications, and afterward was taken to meet General Wood. The impression he made must have been satisfactory. Before the end of the week, he was told the position was his.

Nothing, it turned out, could have suited him better than his job with the commission. For most of the next three years he lived aboard the general's yacht, the *Apo,* and visited every one of the major islands in the vast Philippine archipelago. He made dozens of friends among the Filipinos, learned several local dialects, and became familiar with the customs, manners, and beliefs of many of the Islanders.

As time passed, he found himself thinking less and less about returning to America. In this respect, he knew that he differed from many of his countrymen who had come out to the Islands. Their usual intention was to stay in the Territory for a few years, "make a pile," and then, as soon as they could, take their money and go back to New York or Pennsylvania or California. But after only a few months with the commission, he knew he would never do that. His temperament was suited to the tropics. He already loved the white, curving beaches, the wet jungles, the vast, empty, romantic seas. And he already felt at home among the graceful, polite, good-humored Island people—much more at home than he would have felt back in the States.

The truth was that he had become one of a small band of American expatriates. He had found his future among the tropical Islands.

When his work with the commission was over, Chick Parsons returned to Manila, where he used some of the money he'd saved to pay for a night course in commerce at the University of the Philippines. During the day he worked for the Manila Telephone Company as assistant commercial superintendent. For a year or two he was satisfied to remain in the city, but then he felt the urge to travel again. In 1926, when he was twenty-four, he changed jobs once more, becoming the buyer-manager for Meyer-Muzzall & Company, a firm engaged in the purchase and export of lumber.

After that he spent much of his time in the south, particularly on Mindanao, the second largest island in the Philippines. There, he was responsible for the selection of timber, its transportation to the coast, and its subsequent shipment to the United States. His job brought him to every quarter of the huge island, until he knew as much about the land and the people as anyone could who was not a native himself.

His stay among the islands of the south made him more aware of the widespread Filipino yearning for complete national independence. It also made him more sympathetic to the impatience some Islanders felt toward American officials in Manila and Washington. Long ago the United States had promised the Filipinos their freedom, once they had become sufficiently experienced in the ways of democracy and self-government. The promise had been well intentioned; in the meantime, however, an American governor-general still sat in Manila; the Islands had achieved only the status of a provisional republic; and to some men, at least, the day of independence seemed too far away.

While he remained in the south, other concerns besides politics took up his time. Though born in a small, land-locked American town, he always had felt drawn to the sea. Now he was often on the water, directing the operation of his company's ships and barges. Without being consciously aware of it, he gradually acquired a considerable amount of experience, until finally, in 1929, he decided to put his seamanship to use by joining the Naval Reserve. After that, Lieutenant, junior grade, Charles Parsons went on active duty as often as he could.

The busy, pleasant, footloose years slipped by all too quickly on Mindanao. Then one afternoon, in the city of Zamboanga, he received an invitation to supper. It was from an American named Stephen Jurika, a veteran of the Spanish-American War. Jurika had come to the Philippines as a soldier in 1899, and after the fighting had ended he'd decided to stay on. He had lived in the Islands ever since, for more than thirty years.

At supper that night, Parsons was entertained by Stephen Jurika and his wife, Blanche, and by their son and daughter, Tommy and Katrushka. Afterward he could remember only two things about the evening: Katrushka was called "Katsy" by her family—they pronounced it "Kotsy"—and she was the prettiest girl he had ever seen.

No one appeared surprised when he became a regular visitor at the Jurikas', nor was there any particular astonishment a few weeks later when he and Katsy announced their engagement. Though she was still very young, they were married before the year was out, in Zamboanga.

Marriage brought an end to his wanderings. He and Katsy decided to move to Manila; and not long after the wedding they left for the northernmost island of Luzon, to set up housekeeping in the capital.

The years seemed to pass by even more swiftly there. They had three sons, Michael, Peter, and then Patrick. When Stephen Jurika died, his wife, Blanche, left Zamboanga and came to the capital, to live with them and to help care for her grandchildren.

Business activities in Manila took up much of his time.

He became interested in several enterprises, including the Luzon Stevedoring Company, which owned chrome and manganese mines in the central and southern islands, as well as a fleet of tugboats and other craft based in Manila. In his role of "boss stevedore," Chick Parsons became a familiar figure around the piers and docks of the city, a short, wiry American who was as popular with his Filipino workers as he was with the United States officials at nearby Cavite naval base or those across the bay on the island fortress of Corregidor.

Sometimes, in the evenings, he and Katsy talked about the future. They had no pressing financial worries. Why shouldn't he begin to take things easy? In a few years he could turn some of his responsibilities over to others, and then have more leisure time to spend with his friends and family.

And yet, it was becoming increasingly difficult to speak with any confidence of the days ahead. Local newspapers had begun to describe the European war that now was raging, half a world away. Defenseless cities were being bombed; entire countries were being overrun by enemy armies. How long could America and her overseas territories remain at peace? How long would it be before violence and bloodshed spread to the western Pacific and the Philippines?

2

PEACE AND WAR

BY 1941, IT WAS NO LONGER POSSIBLE TO AVOID SEEING
the danger signs, even in remote and tranquil Manila. For
almost a decade Japan, the Pacific's most warlike and ambitious nation, had been on the march. As far back as 1931,
Japanese armies had invaded Manchuria. They had
launched a further attack against mainland China in 1932.
Since then, relations between Japan and the United States
had grown increasingly tense in the Pacific, as the two
countries drifted closer to what some men believed was
inevitable conflict.

In Europe, Japan's political allies, Germany and Italy,
had been rattling their sabers for almost an equal length of
time. Hostilities finally had begun in the autumn of 1939.

Less than a year later, Hitler's German armies had swept over Norway, the Low Countries, and France, until in western Europe only the British remained free to oppose the Nazi scourge. Soon, the war had spread to the Balkans and Russia; North Africa and the Mediterranean Sea had become fiercely contested battlegrounds.

Through all this, only one major power in the world had remained "neutral." Technically, the United States was still at peace, and life in her overseas territories had gone on with deceptive serenity.

In their Manila household, the Parsons met frequently with friends and discussed world affairs, the distant war in Europe, and the infinitely closer menace of Imperial Japan. They talked, too, of conditions in the States, and how the government was finally making a belated effort to strengthen its long-neglected military and naval forces; in the Atlantic, America was giving aid to her beleaguered British friends "by every means short of war"; in the Pacific, there was a new and strict embargo on the sale of vital oil and scrap metal to Japan, materials the government in Tokyo desperately needed for future operations. In the presence of such global conflicts and dangers, could any large, uncommitted nation hope to remain on the sidelines very much longer?

By the beginning of December, 1941, there was a sense of approaching crisis in Manila. High-flying Japanese planes had been observed over both the capital and the peninsula of Bataan to the north. Such flights were extremely disquieting; they implied that the Japanese "were up to something"—but the question remained—exactly what?

Still, some of the guests who came to visit the Parsons confidently insisted that the crisis would pass and that there would be no war. They pointed to the fact that two leading Japanese diplomats were even then in Washington, presenting their government's views on the American embargo and the general situation in the Pacific. The Japanese were holding discussions with President Roosevelt and Cordell Hull, the United States Secretary of State, in order to negotiate a reasonable settlement between the two countries—and most likely, such a settlement would soon be reached.

Of course, if negotiations failed, then certainly grave difficulties could be anticipated. But the real danger would not arise for a while yet, probably not for another six months or a year, at which time the Japanese might become truly desperate for oil and scrap iron.

Their visitors explained that there was no immediate reason for concern, at least not while peace talks were still continuing in Washington. Besides, the Japanese were too clever to get into a war with the United States. They knew America's real strength. Though only partly rearmed, her forces would be too much for the Japanese; the government in Tokyo was aware of its own weakness. After almost ten years of fighting, the emperor's armies still had not been able to subdue China, a third-class power. So, if the Japanese knew what was good for them, they would reach some kind of peaceful arrangement with Washington, and make every effort to get back on the right side of Uncle Sam.

As for their own situation here in Manila—well, it was hard to see why there was any particular cause for alarm. Even if war should come, the Islands' defensive forces could easily handle things. There were plenty of American Regular Army troops available; there were the Philippine Scouts in support; there were some United States Marines, recently brought back from their Shanghai station; and there were also a great many Filipino recruits, just called up to the colors a few weeks ago. All these regiments and battalions, equipped with American arms, and supported by American planes, would easily drive any Japanese invasion force back into the sea.

There was a crisis, of course, a serious one—but what was the point of being so anxious about it?

Chick Parsons did not attempt to argue with his guests, but he remained unimpressed by their optimism. From time to time, at the Army and Navy Club, he had talked with high-ranking military and naval officers. Their off-the-record remarks were not encouraging.

It was believed that the Japanese had as many as three thousand first-line combat planes stationed on the island of Formosa, six hundred miles to the north of Manila. That would place them within easy bombing range of the city's docks, the naval base at nearby Cavite, and the neighboring airfields around the city and those on Bataan peninsula. To oppose the Japanese, General Douglas MacArthur could call on about three hundred planes, many of them either trainers or near-obsolete fighters. In the event of war, the enemy, at least initially, would control the air.

The situation at sea looked equally unpromising. America's main naval strength was based at Pearl Harbor, far to the east, in the Hawaiian Islands. At Cavite there was a small flotilla of American submarines, but little else. The Japanese Navy commanded the western Pacific, including all Philippine waters. If they chose to, they could land an invasion army of several battle-hardened divisions, equipped with the most modern armaments, and could do so, almost certainly, without much effective opposition. Once ashore in the Islands, they would face a combined American-Filipino defense force that would be vastly inferior in weapons and training, and quite possibly in numbers as well.

The truth was that the Islands were ill-prepared for war. Washington's strict adherence to past disarmament treaties that the Japanese had violated, plus years of apathy and neglect, had left the Philippines in an exposed position. If fighting broke out, as it could at any time, the situation might soon prove to be far more grim than most American civilians had anticipated.

On December 8, 1941, Parsons was aroused from sleep in the dead of night. Someone was knocking at the front door. He switched on a light and looked at his watch. It was 2:30 A.M.

Downstairs, he found a naval officer from the Port Commander's office in Manila. The officer had come with unbelievable news. While their diplomats were still in Washington, "talking peace," the Japanese had launched an all-out surprise attack against Hawaii.

Parsons changed to a navy uniform, and as they drove to the customs area where he was assigned, he listened to more details. The Japanese had bombed the American base at Pearl Harbor. There had been no warning. Units of the main United States Fleet had been hit, but no one in Manila was certain yet how severe the damage had been.

Airfields on Hawaii also had been attacked. The Japanese had used an aircraft carrier task force, launching their planes while still far at sea. Their naval vessels must have left the home islands of Japan many days earlier. No one had foreseen the possibility of a sneak attack on Hawaii. . . . There was confusion in Washington, at Pearl Harbor, in Manila. . . . It was said that President Roosevelt was going to address Congress, and of course, before long, there would be a formal declaration of war. . . .

Parsons reported to Commander Portz, and was sworn into active service as a lieutenant senior grade, his current rank. He was told that the Luzon Stevedoring Company was now "a part of the U.S. Navy." Every ship in Manila, every tug and barge, would be needed. He was to begin work under navy direction, on an emergency footing, using all available personnel.

Completely stunned, he drove back home in the dark. He had known that at any moment fighting might start, yet now that it had, he found the fact difficult to believe. No one was ready for it. The Islands weren't prepared for war. People didn't know what to expect. In Manila, there were no air-raid shelters to protect civilians. There were hardly any antiaircraft guns to drive off enemy planes.

Daylight came as he was telling the news to Katsy and

her mother. Then they all began to eat breakfast together. Mike and Pete were excited by the talk of war, but Patrick was just a baby, and didn't understand what was being said.

It was a strange meal. Before they had finished, he heard a sound that none of the others had heard before. Bombs were falling, beyond the city, to the north. A slight tremor ran under their feet as they pushed back their chairs.

Outside, he thought he could see a flight of planes, high up and far away. When the boys asked him what was happening, he hesitated. Then he said he wasn't sure—but he believed the first enemy attack already had come.

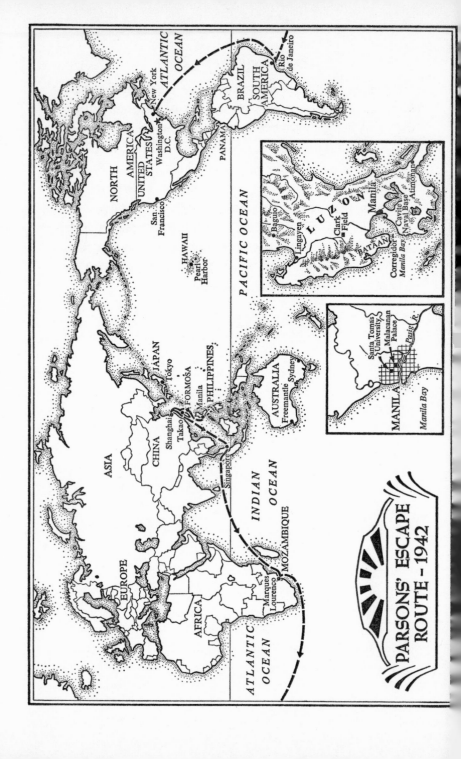

PARSONS' ESCAPE
ROUTE – 1942

3

THE FALL
OF MANILA

SHORTLY AFTER SUNRISE ON DECEMBER 8, 1941, THE
Japanese began a number of devastating air raids against
the island of Luzon. The enemy's first target was Clark Field
outside Manila. Two preliminary attacks did moderate
damage. At 1:30 P.M. the Japanese planes returned.

Inexplicably, eighteen American B-17's, more than half
the heavy bombers stationed in the Islands, were parked in
neat rows on the field. Within minutes, all eighteen either
were burning or had been blown to pieces.

In the north, a similar raid on the same afternoon destroyed almost three-quarters of the American fighter
planes on Luzon. Like the bombers at Clark Field, these
planes were caught on the ground.

The following morning Manila's waterfront was subjected to its first bombing. Soon, clouds of black smoke drifted over the capital. When Japanese planes resumed their attacks the next day, no American defenders rose to meet them. Only forty-eight hours had elapsed since the initial assault, but already the small American air force on Luzon had been virtually annihilated.

During the month of December, all American military and naval personnel worked around the clock in Manila. Chick Parsons found himself assigned to the Port Commander's Office in the Port Terminal Building. His duties were many and varied. At night, American submarines crept into the docks to refuel under the cover of darkness, and it was his responsibility to see that sufficient quantities of oil were on hand when the subs tied up. He also helped to remove supplies from warehouses along the waterfront, supervised their loading, and then ran them across the open bay to the American and Filipino troops on Bataan and Corregidor.

One afternoon, in his office, he received a curious request. Several Danish ships had been caught in Manila at the outbreak of hostilities. Unless they were transferred to the flag of a neutral nation, the Japanese were sure to seize them as prizes of war when they sailed from port. The decision had been made to change them from Danish to Panamanian registry. The difficulty was this: Neutral Panama did not have an official diplomatic representative in the Philippine capital who could accept title to the vessels. However, during the past six or seven years, Parsons occasionally had acted as a sort of "honorary" Consul of Panama. Now he was asked if he would be willing to become the "official" Consul, and take possession of the ships on behalf of the Panamanian Government.

Parsons said that he would be glad to cooperate, and not long afterward the transfer of ships was completed. Later he received a diplomatic passport. The Philippine authorities also entered his name in their records as the "official" Consul of the Republic of Panama. All of this was only a legalistic fiction, designed to save a number of Danish ships, and the incident soon slipped from his mind.

Having gained almost complete control of the air, the Japanese began their invasion of Luzon during the fourth week of December. The enemy's aim was to capture Manila, and destroy American-Filipino resistance on the largest and most important island of the Philippines.

Two major landings were made. The first came at Atimonan, to the southeast of Manila, the second at Lingayen, to the northwest. In the north, the hills of Bataan offered the best terrain for defense. As resistance began to crumble in the south, General MacArthur decided to abandon Manila itself and make a stand with his troops on Bataan. The fortress of Corregidor, offshore from the southern tip of the peninsula, was selected as his new headquarters.

On December 24th, MacArthur arrived at the island-fortress. He was accompanied by several important civilian officials, men who could help to establish a Philippine Government-in-Exile, if that step should become necessary. In his party were Francis Sayre, the United States High

Commissioner, Philippine President Manuel Quezon; and Philippine Vice-President Sergio Osmeña. Only a skeleton staff was left behind in Manila. To spare the civilian population, the capital was declared an open city. No effort would be made to defend it or to impede the entrance of the enemy soldiers now approaching from the south.

For a week, Chick Parsons slept scarcely at all. From Christmas Day until New Year's Eve, Manila's naval and military installations had to be destroyed lest they fall intact into Japanese hands. At the same time, supplies had to be ferried at a frantic pace to Bataan and Corregidor.

The most important installation marked for destruction was the naval base at Cavite. On Christmas Night, explosive charges were placed and detonated. A series of violent explosions shattered the still evening. Flames rose hundreds of feet, illuminating the vast bay. As Cavite burned, Americans like Chick Parsons knew that they were witnessing the end of their country's naval prestige in the western Pacific and that it might be a long time indeed before it could be restored.

On December 30th, the Japanese advance had reached a point only five miles south of Manila. By then, many of the defenders had retired to the north, some to hide in the hills, some to join in the defense of Bataan.

Manila itself was a bewildered and desolate city. For days there had been scattered fires, particularly in the port area near the piers. Demolition work continued, and the blasts, destroying military and naval stores, could be felt day and night, even in distant residential districts.

Much of Manila had been spared heavy bombing because the Japanese realized the capital would soon be theirs, and they had no wish to occupy a badly damaged city. There had been a few light raids, though. During one, several low-flying planes had destroyed the historic and well-loved Church of Santo Domingo. The raid, made after Manila had been declared an open city, increased the sense of rage and helplessness that both the Americans and Filipinos felt in the doomed capital.

By New Year's Eve, almost all of Chick Parsons' work was done. Cavite Naval Base was a charred and blackened ruin. Warehouses had been emptied of military equipment, food, and medical supplies, and these had been transported across the bay to Corregidor. The Japanese would soon be making their entrance into the city. The moment had come to perform his last duties, and to welcome the New Year with a final grim ceremony.

Katsy insisted on accompanying him, and as the daylight faded, they drove together to the port. They made a strange-looking couple, she in an evening gown and high heels, he in a dirty, sweat-stained navy uniform.

Leaving their car, they walked slowly along the docks. At each pier, a group of shadowy figures emerged from the darkness. Parsons greeted his men, talked with them briefly, then gave an order. Rags soaked in gasoline were lighted. Small charges were set off. With every explosion another of the city's commercial warehouses, crammed full of a thousand items of peacetime commerce, began to go up in flames.

Finally, near the Army and Navy Club, they came to the

last undamaged dock. A crowded ferry was there, ready to cast off. Aboard they saw several of their friends, including naval officers, newspaper reporters, and other Americans from the city. They were taking the final boat to "impregnable" Corregidor and to what they imagined was safety from the Japanese. Almost tearfully, they begged Chick and Katsy Parsons to join them. It was suicide or worse to stay in Manila. Everyone knew how the Japanese had shot defenseless civilians in China, how General Homma and his soldiers had committed unspeakable atrocities in the city of Nanking. And now, the same General Homma was approaching the capital. . . .

Parsons shook his head. He was going to stick it out in Manila. Somehow, by hook or crook, he'd manage to look after Katsy and her mother and the three Parsons children.

The crowded ferry pulled away from the dock. When it had reached a safe distance, waiting men stepped out of the shadows again. *"Ahora, Capitán?"* they asked. "Now, Captain?"

"Ahora, amigos," Chick Parsons replied. He shook hands with his Filipino workmen, and said goodbye. As the last pier was put to the torch, he and Katsy walked over to the nearby Army and Navy Club. From the veranda they could see a dozen fires raging along the waterfront. It was almost midnight. They went inside the club, and he put a coin in the jukebox. A clock struck the hour, signaling the New Year, as they waltzed slowly and sadly around the deserted room.

When he had no more change to put in the jukebox, he

left Katsy and went to his locker, where he gathered up the rest of his khaki uniforms. It was time to start thinking about destroying his navy gear and becoming a civilian again. For if the Japanese learned that he was a naval officer, he would be taken to a military prison, while Katsy and the others went to a civilian internment camp. Should that happen, he would not be able to protect them, and any future chance the Parsons family might have of escaping from the Islands would be reduced almost to zero.

The following day he got up at dawn and built a bonfire behind the house, in a corner of the yard. Then he soaked his suntan jackets, shirts, and pants in gasoline. One after another, he threw them into the flames. They burned fiercely, until they had been reduced to a heap of glowing ashes. But afterward the brass buttons, though darkened and charred, could still be identified as United States Navy insignia. They had to be disposed of, in a place where they couldn't be found.

When the fire had grown cold, he and Katsy gathered up all the buttons, and then took them out to the car. They drove to an island in the Pasig River, and dropped the buttons into the water. It wasn't long before the last one had disappeared in the swift current, and Lieutenant Charles Parsons, U.S.N.R., had reverted to plain Chick Parsons.

On the way home, they saw something puzzling. A block or two from the Japanese Club, a crowd stood lining the street. Flags were being waved—flags of the Rising Sun. Most of the men and women in the crowd were Japanese, undoubtedly native born, who were all too happy at the prospect of the emperor's soldiers taking over the city. There were also a few Filipinos standing among them, probably turncoats, or those utterly terrified of the invaders.

But what the crowd was doing there Parsons couldn't have said. Until that moment he had been sure the Japanese were not planning to enter Manila until the following morning.

Then he heard the sound of a band, coming from the direction of Taft Avenue. At the next cross street, two civilian guards wearing Japanese armbands leaped onto the running boards.

"We are commandeering this car to drive to Parañaque," they said.

"What for?" Parsons asked them.

"To meet the Honorable General Homma. He is coming at the head of a victory parade that will show the ignorant and uninformed how great is the glory of the emperor."

Parsons had no intention of driving to the suburbs to pick up the notorious General Homma, and then acting as his chauffeur during the enemy's triumphal entrance into the capital. Quietly he told Katsy to be ready when he gave the signal.

"This city," he said to the civilian guards, "may be Japanese tomorrow. It's still American today."

He nodded to Katsy. At the same instant, they shoved, left and right. The astonished guards fell off the running boards, into the street. Parsons pressed his foot on the accelerator, and their car sped away.

Behind them, there were shouts and curses. Then some badly aimed bullets whined through the air. Luckily, the

guards had no car. After swinging wildly around a corner
or two, Parsons saw that they were not being pursued, and
in another few minutes they were safely back at their house.

By the next morning the Japanese had taken possession
of Manila, and for the first time in several weeks there was
no sound of bombs exploding or of demolition charges
being set off by the docks.

There were other changes, too. Much less pleasant ones.
When Parsons got up and looked from the window, he saw
a Japanese soldier on sentry duty by their front gate.

After a wash and shave, he dressed, and then walked
outside to have a look around. There was a sign on the
fence, bearing Japanese characters. Katsy and her mother
came out, too. Both women had lived for a brief time in
Japan, and could read and speak the language a little.

The sign said: "Property of the Imperial Japanese Government." Their house had been confiscated; before long,
like other American civilians trapped in Manila, they would
be picked up and driven to an internment camp. The local
authorities already had completed the necessary arrangements. The camp was to be located at Santo Tomás, inside
the fifty-two-acre walled campus of the university. Though
facilities there would be greatly overtaxed, the campus was
by far the best site available in the city for a civilian prison.

When breakfast was over, Katsy and her mother began to
pack the few possessions the family would be allowed to
take with them. They had scarcely finished when a Japanese
truck drove along the street. It stopped in front of the
house. Two armed Japanese soldiers climbed out and

started up the walk. As Parsons watched them approach, an idea suddenly occurred to him. It was a long shot—but it might just work.

"You know," he said to Katsy, "they *can't* lock me up. I'm a neutral diplomat—with diplomatic immunity. I happen to be the Panamanian Consul."

"But you're not a *real* consul," Katsy said. "You were just given some official papers because of those Danish ships."

"Real or not," he said, "do you think our Japanese friends are likely to know the difference?"

It took him only seconds to reach his desk, where he found his diplomatic passport and seals of office. He gave them to Katsy and her mother, and then sent the two women down to the front door to talk with the soldiers. "I'll be there in a minute," he told them. "First, I want to look for something else up here."

The seals and passport puzzled the soldiers. While they were expressing their doubts, young Mike Parsons appeared. He was eight years old. All he understood was that two of the enemy were standing at the door, threatening his family. He shouted at the soldiers: "You can't take us to a concentration camp! My dad's an officer in the United States Navy!"

Mike and Pete, the two oldest Parsons boys, knew as much Spanish as English. Fortunately, this time Mike had spoken in Spanish, a language few Japanese soldiers understood. He didn't have a chance to try again in English. His grandmother hurried him away to another room, and quickly explained what they could and could not say, now that the Japanese held the city.

Katsy was still arguing with the soldiers by the front door when Parsons came downstairs with additional proof. He had found a number of flags among the children's toys, and one of them happened to be the flag of Panama.

He and Katsy smiled at the soldiers. Then, carrying the flag carefully so that it didn't touch the ground, they went outside to the front of the house and ran it up the flagpole. The soldiers seemed impressed with the ceremony. They bowed gravely, looked at the flag fluttering on the pole, and finally went back to their truck.

An hour later two Japanese civilians drove up in a car. They explained politely that they wished to see "the Panamanian Consul's credentials." Once again the seals of office and the passport were brought out. The officials inspected them. They looked closely at Parsons. He was short and dark, and just then, happened to be very sunburned. He could easily have been mistaken for a citizen of one of the Central American republics.

The officials examined the seals and the passport a second time. They said that everything seemed to be in order but that they would look into the matter further. Then they would return.

The next day the two officials reappeared. If anything, they were even more polite. They said that the files of the Philippine Government at Malacanan Palace had been inspected and that Charles Parsons was indeed registered there as the Panamanian Consul. Of course, as the accredited representative of a neutral nation he would receive all the usual diplomatic courtesies. He and his family could remain where they were, in their own house, with their own servants. The Japanese Government was extremely civilized. It knew how to deal with its enemies, and with its friends.

The Japanese officials rose, bowed several times, and drove away in their car.

During the afternoon Parsons had a sign made for the house. He put it on the fence. Written in Japanese characters, the sign said that the house was the Official Consulate of Panama and that Charles Parsons, the Panamanian Consul, was in residence there.

Temporarily, they had escaped imprisonment. But how long they could keep up the deception was anyone's guess. And it wasn't pleasant to think what the Japanese would do if they ever discovered that Charles Parsons was really a United States Naval officer, and the man who had destroyed most of the warehouses and piers on Manila Bay.

4

THE INTELLIGENCE FILE

THERE WAS LITTLE FOR MOST AMERICANS TO CHEER about in the Philippines during the early weeks of 1942. At first it was believed that the swift loss of Manila and the retreat to Bataan were merely temporary setbacks and that soon a powerful force of planes, ships, and troops would appear in the Islands to drive out the Japanese invaders.

In time these extravagant illusions began to fade. Help was not coming because it simply didn't exist. The American Pacific Fleet had been gravely damaged at Pearl Harbor; combat-ready divisions were few, and were needed elsewhere; scarce aircraft had to be conserved until factories on the mainland could enter full production and thousands of additional pilots could be trained to fly the new planes. In the meantime, American and Filipino soldiers, encircled on Bataan and Corregidor, gazed in vain at the horizon. Their ammunition and other necessities already in short supply, the defenders realized the situation was desperate. They were surrounded, without any real hope of rescue or relief.

For Chick Parsons, life in occupied Manila was now a precarious affair. By acting on impulse, and assuming the guise of a Central American diplomat, he had greatly increased the danger to himself and his family. True, he had kept them all out of prison thus far. But literally hundreds of people in the city knew his real identity, and if even one of them chose to betray him to the Kempeitai, the brutal Japanese secret police, then certainly he himself, and possibly even Katsy and the children, would be tortured and killed.

On the other hand, there was at least one reason for guarded optimism. A rumor had begun to circulate that an agreement would soon be reached between the Japanese Government and the neutral countries of Latin America. The agreement would call for an exchange of civilians: Latin American families now stranded in the Philippines would be allowed to return to their homelands, while Japanese families in Latin America would go back to Japan. Before long, Parsons paid a visit to Malacanan Palace, and made inquiries. No one there knew if a final agreement would be concluded, but apparently such an exchange was being seriously discussed.

Parsons said Yes, he and his family wished to return to

Panama as quickly as possible. Their names were added to a list of neutral civilians requesting repatriation. In another few weeks the "Panamanian Consul" and his family might be out of the country, and that would be far better than rotting for the rest of the war, or starving to death, in a Japanese internment camp.

The prospect of escaping from the Islands encouraged Parsons to consider new plans. His position in Manila was unique. He was probably the only American in the capital who could gather information, with a reasonable chance of presenting it shortly to the authorities back in the States. The opportunity was too good to miss. He was by no means certain what sort of reports Washington might desire, but after considering the problem for several days he decided that an accurate picture of local conditions would undoubtedly be useful.

He and Katsy began to assemble an intelligence file. Into it went daily copies of the Japanese-run newspaper, the Manila *Tribune,* first published after the fall of the capital. To these were added samples of surrender leaflets, dropped on the countryside, and examples of Japanese paper money, printed especially for the Philippine occupation.

Still, Parsons felt dissatisfied. He was certain that somehow he ought to be accomplishing more. As a neutral diplomat he'd found he could move around the city with considerable freedom. Cautiously, he began to reestablish contact with trusted Filipino friends, and then even with those whom he had known more casually. He felt reasonably safe in doing so, because he was certain of one thing—

hardly anyone in Manila had much use for the invaders or for their program of "an Orient for the Orientals," the so-called "Co-Prosperity Sphere," which the Japanese Ministry of Propaganda had been shrilly promoting during the past decade.

The fact was that many Islanders had long mistrusted the intentions of their powerful neighbors to the north. Now their worst fears were realized. The Japanese had come as arrogant and ruthless invaders, and most Filipinos harbored a passionate hatred of the conquerors.

There was something else that made the arrival of the Japanese seem even more galling. The United States had promised that in 1945, just three years hence, the Islanders would finally attain their complete independence. It was a numbing blow to many Filipinos to see their country over-run, after so many years of patient waiting, and with freedom so near at hand.

Gradually, through his network of friends in the city, Chick Parsons began to hear talk of a new kind. There were growing reports of unsurrendered soldiers and sailors in the hills of Luzon, many still armed with rifles, pistols, and ammunition. Some were Americans, some Filipinos. All apparently considered themselves capable of resistance, and had no intention of surrendering to the enemy.

With great care, Parsons sent out requests for further, more detailed, information. Innocent-looking Filipinos began to appear at the back door of his house. Mostly they were vendors and peddlers, hawking a mixture of wares. They brought scraps of news about the men in the hills, their location, their numbers, their arms, their possible plans.

Parsons' interest grew stronger. He knew that Washington would want to learn as much as possible about the situation, and he began to consider whether it might not be desirable to go out and investigate matters himself.

By now he had grown quite accustomed to moving around inside the enemy-held city. Only once had there been any trouble. Early one afternoon he'd been arrested, and taken to Santo Tomás prison. After an hour or two, the police had examined his papers and listened to his explanation of the "official business" he'd been pursuing. No one really was suspicious, though. It turned out to be a routine affair, and he'd got back home in time for supper, before Katsy and her mother had begun to worry or before Mike and Peter had begun to ask where he was.

Having thought the matter over carefully, he decided that an occasional excursion into the hills would not be too dangerous. Such trips would have to be kept brief, though. The Japanese might appear at the house at any time, and a prolonged absence on his part would probably arouse their suspicions. And though he didn't like the idea, he knew that he would have to travel in disguise, because there simply was no reason for the Panamanian Consul to be wandering around the villages of Luzon, questioning the local inhabitants.

Unobtrusively, a barefoot "peasant" wearing old clothes and a straw hat began to shuffle away from the consulate, to reappear several hours later in the distant hills. Riding on lumbering carts, following remote trails on foot, Chick Parsons made his round. He discovered men living in caves or holed up in small villages at the end of narrow, almost inaccessible trails. They had little in common except their arms and the determination not to give themselves up to the Japanese. Some were businessmen from Manila, who had chosen hardship and freedom rather than collaboration with the enemy. Some were officers whose battalions and regiments had been scattered and overwhelmed. Others were enlisted men who had become separated from their units during the attempt to reach Bataan and Corregidor. Among them were farmers, schoolteachers, civil servants, and not a few who were bandits and cutthroats.

As yet they had no organization or plans for coordinated resistance. Each man was concerned almost exclusively with protecting himself and his family. Only a few of the officers were beginning to think ahead, to wonder if some kind of unified activity might be possible. While talking with these officers, the idea first occurred to Parsons that one day a guerrilla movement might be formed among the unsurrendered forces in the Islands. Clearly, though, the time was not ripe to launch such a movement from the villages of Luzon.

For the most part the men he talked with seemed to be thinking only in terms of outside help. They had heard President Roosevelt's voice on the radio, promising that one day aid would be sent. The word itself was beginning to have an almost magical significance to the people in the countryside. The "aid"—the American President in Washington had promised it. When would the "aid" come?

These were the worst moments he experienced, during

his brief excursions outside the capital. Because he really had no answer for the men in the hills.

As the weeks passed in Manila, Chick Parsons became convinced that the President's promised assistance would not reach the Islands for a long, long time. The United States and her allies were hard pressed everywhere in the Southwest Pacific. Singapore, Great Britain's strongest Far Eastern base, had surrendered to the Japanese. The enemy had made successful landings in the Dutch East Indies, and was rapidly overcoming allied resistance there. Australia was threatened with a possible invasion, and Burma and even India were no longer considered safe.

In the isolated Philippines, now completely bypassed by the Japanese sweep to the south and west, there were signs that the fighting was not expected to last much longer. During February, high-ranking civilian officials secretly left Corregidor and boarded a submarine. Their destination was distant Australia, their ultimate aim to establish a Philippine Government-in-Exile.

One day in mid-March, General MacArthur received orders from Washington to make a similar departure. Arriving safely in Australia, he issued a promise that soon became a legend throughout the Islands. The United States, he said, had not forgotten its loyal ally. As quickly as possible, American forces would come back to help the Philippine people. The land would again be free, and the Islanders would enjoy at last the full independence that had been pledged so long ago. The general's famous words were: "I shall return."

But the very fact of his departure made it clear that the troops on Bataan and Corregidor were now fighting a delaying action and that organized resistance on Luzon was almost over. On April 9th, the gallant forces trapped on the peninsula, mercilessly pounded by a larger and better-equipped army, without adequate medical supplies, their ammunition nearly gone, finally laid down their arms. Only the fortress of Corregidor refused to yield.

News of Bataan's surrender, one of the greatest defeats in United States military history, quickly reached Manila. It was followed by something almost too horrible to believe. For several days, under a tropical sun, thousands of American prisoners, many of them wounded, almost all without food or water, were compelled to march northward to prison camps in the hills. The victorious Japanese behaved barbarously. Men who could not keep up with the march because of wounds or exhaustion were bayoneted, bludgeoned, or shot to death by the side of the road. No one knew how many died before the tragedy was over, but the Death March from Bataan was not quickly forgotten by those Filipinos who witnessed it from their villages and farms. Nor was it forgotten by the citizens of Manila. Numerous soldiers on Bataan had been serving in the Islands for many years, and during their tours of duty they had married into Filipino families. The treatment of these men—some friends, some relatives by marriage—did nothing to soften the Islanders' hatred of the enemy.

Less than two weeks after the fall of Bataan, on April 18, 1942, a Japanese patrol came to the Panamanian Consulate.

The soldiers marched up to the front door, burst into the house without knocking, and told Chick Parsons he was under arrest.

Before he was forced to leave, he and Katsy exchanged a wordless glance. Both of them knew this was no routine affair. He was in the gravest danger. From the violently angry appearance of the guards there was every reason to fear that his identity had been discovered and that now he was being led away to execution.

5

AFTER CORREGIDOR

WITHIN MINUTES OF HIS ARREST, KATSY PARSONS TRIED to find out if there was anything she could do to help her husband. Through one of their many friends in the city she quickly discovered his whereabouts. The news was grim. This time he had not been taken to the civilian internment camp at Santa Tomás, but instead had been driven directly to the old Spanish prison of Fort Santiago, a place where only the most important prisoners were kept.

Abandoned for many years, Fort Santiago had been used by the Japanese secret police since the fall of Manila. In those few months it had gained an evil reputation. It was whispered that many prisoners who walked through the gates never walked out again. There were dungeons in the old fort, and ancient instruments of torture. But the ruthless agents of the Kempeitai did not rely exclusively on such old-fashioned methods. They knew a dozen modern ways to loosen a man's tongue. One of the most effective was said to be their infamous "water cure." When it was used with moderation, a prisoner could be kept alive for weeks. When it was used without restraint, it could easily kill a man in one or two agonizing hours.

Despite all this, Katsy Parsons was told, there were strong reasons to remain hopeful. Clearly, her husband had not been singled out for punishment. Though as yet there was no explanation for it, apparently every other consular official who represented a neutral western nation had been arrested that day too.

There was more to the puzzle. Seemingly, something had happened to enrage the conquerors of Manila. Overnight the Japanese had dropped their characteristic mask of cold, formal politeness, to behave instead like a gang of violent savages. All non-Orientals appearing on the streets that morning had been cursed and beaten by the police. Nor had the assaults been directed solely against Westerners. Scores of ordinary Filipinos were reported under arrest. The police had come, shouted angrily, and hauled them away.

Without doubt, Katsy was reassured, the reason for all this would become known before very long. In the meantime, since her husband had been only one of many taken into custody, there was every likelihood he was still all right and would soon be released.

On the same evening a radio broadcast over the Japanese propaganda station made the matter clear. The announcer, almost hysterical with anger, shouted that Tokyo, the capital of Japan, had been attacked by American planes. A flight of bombers had flown over the unsuspecting city. The "cowardly" pilots had dropped their missiles and then disappeared in the direction of unoccupied China. Behind them, the announcer raved, they had left "scores" of hospitals and churches destroyed, and "many hundreds" of innocent women and children dead and dying.

To anyone who understood the Japanese people, their fury over a single, limited raid was not surprising. For centuries Japanese tradition had attached the greatest importance to "saving face," to the avoidance, at nearly any cost, of public humiliation. The handful of bombs dropped on its supposedly invulnerable capital by Colonel James Doolittle's daring raiders had subjected the entire Japanese nation, in its own view, to just such a humiliation. Damaged pride had sparked the violence in Manila, the abuse of non-Orientals, the arrest of neutral diplomats. But how long such hysterical anger might last, or how many victims it might claim before subsiding, no one in the Philippine capital could say.

It seemed ages before Katsy learned that her husband was still alive. The Japanese had not released him, however. Instead they had transferred him from Fort Santiago to the internment camp at Santo Tomás, where she knew that at least he would receive more humane treatment.

Another friend of theirs, a Filipino doctor, was granted permission to visit Parsons in Santo Tomás. Later, the doctor came to the house. Chick was all right, he reported to

Katsy. He was tough. He had withstood whatever treatment the Japanese had used, in their efforts to make him give information after his arrest.

Reluctantly the doctor confessed that her husband undoubtedly had been tortured. There were external signs . . . the fingernails of his right hand. . . . And there were internal indications, too . . . particularly his kidneys. . . . Yes, Chick hadn't wanted to talk about his experiences, but it seemed all too likely that the secret police had given him several doses of their "water cure" in the Fort Santiago dungeons. Still, all things considered, he was in quite good condition. After a couple of weeks' rest, he believed her husband would be as fit as ever.

In a few days the doctor arranged to have his patient transferred to a hospital in Manila. The first time Katsy visited him, she saw how unusually pale he looked—and she noticed that the fingernails of his right hand were just beginning to grow back in again. But she didn't ask him about it, and he didn't volunteer any information. Whatever his reasons, he seemed to want to remain silent on the subject of Fort Santiago. So, by unspoken agreement, they acted as though he had never been in the custody of the secret police.

Despite the doctor's optimism, Parsons did not recover quickly. To speed his recuperation, the doctor obtained permission for him to return home for a week. Katsy and Blanche Jurika could care for him there, and he could see Mike, Pete, and Patrick the baby again.

During his week at home the last American forces on Luzon laid down their arms. Late in May, 1942, the surrender of battered and beleaguered Corregidor was announced in the city; not long afterward, other American troops scattered throughout the Islands were compelled to capitulate because of the enemy's threat to massacre all of Corregidor's prisoners if resistance continued elsewhere.

From their own porch, the Parsons family saw the dismal aftermath of Corregidor's surrender. Seven thousand battle-weary American prisoners, many of them gaunt with fatigue, dozens of them wounded and delirious, were forced to stagger through the streets of the capital under the remorseless prodding of Japanese guards. The enemy's aim was to humiliate the former rulers of the country, and by doing so, to impress the Filipinos with the strength of Japanese arms. Instead, they succeeded in stiffening even further the Islanders' will to resist. For many of those in the watching crowds saw friends passing or recognized the American soldier they knew who had married a Filipino girl in Davao, Manila, or Zamboanga. And when sympathetic Manilans tried to hand a piece of fruit or a cup of water to one of the wretched prisoners, the guards jabbed them with bayonets and drove them away.

A day or two after the grisly parade was over, Parsons began to review the latest newspapers and other material that Katsy and her mother had managed to collect during his imprisonment. With the end of organized resistance in the Islands, their intelligence file seemed to have taken on even greater value. Certainly Washington and the outside world would have no accurate idea of present conditions in the Philippines. The only "facts" available were those being offered by Japanese propaganda broadcasts, at best a highly prejudiced and inaccurate source of information.

Corregidor's fall also meant that numerous American servicemen were now being moved to prisons in and around Manila. To relieve the uncertainty and despair of their relatives back in the States, Parsons decided to learn who they were, and to add a list of their names to the file. Another friend of theirs, a courageous priest, already had been granted permission to visit some of the prisoners. Each day he brought out a few more names and serial numbers, while Katsy and her mother obtained still others during their comings and goings around Santo Tomás.

When his week's home leave was up, Parsons was taken back to confinement in the civilian prison. He went with deep misgivings. It was difficult to understand why the Japanese refused to give him his release. Perhaps their insane hatred of all Westerners was part of the explanation. Perhaps he was under active suspicion. Or perhaps the Tokyo raid still rankled so bitterly that the emperor's government no longer cared whether or not it offended neutral diplomats by acting in defiance of international law. If such were the case, it was a bad omen. Because if the Japanese were angry enough, they might very well decide not to conclude the civilian exchange on which he had been counting so heavily all these past months.

Two more dreary weeks passed in confinement, without any word from the police authorities. Then, well after dark on the evening of June 4th, he was ordered to report to the prison commandant. Inside the office stood a member of the Kempeitai.

Parsons was told that secret orders had just arrived. In less than twelve hours, the Panamanian Consul, his wife, mother-in-law, and three children had to be ready to leave Manila, to start the first leg of their trip home. The officer informed Parsons that he and his family would be permitted to take only two pieces of luggage, a steamer trunk and a small suitcase. They were to tell no one that they were being exchanged for Japanese civilians now in Latin America. The first part of their journey would take them to Formosa. No further information could be given them at present about the rest of their itinerary.

One other item, the agent said, should be noted carefully. His wife already had been warned that, on pain of death, they were not to try to take out any printed matter, written material, personal letters, or the like, that might in any way aid or assist the enemies of Japan. A person caught trying to smuggle such things through Customs would be executed on the spot.

Hearing this, Parsons assumed that by now Katsy and her mother had destroyed the intelligence file they all had gone to such lengths to collect. The two women would have done so reluctantly, but the danger of keeping the file would have left them no choice—and he thought no more about the newspapers and other material they had been gathering since the fall of Manila.

A few minutes later he was escorted from the camp and driven home under guard. In the living room he saw the trunk and suitcase, and knew Katsy and her mother had finished packing. He also sensed that something was wrong.

Then Blanche Jurika said in a quiet voice: "I'm not going with you, Chick. Manila is my home. Besides, only yesterday I finally heard about Tommy. He's been taken prisoner on Cebu. As long as my son is there, in a Japanese camp, how could I possibly think of leaving?"

They found that nothing could change Blanche Jurika's mind. Though they argued and pleaded, she only shook her head. And so, just at dawn, they climbed inside the waiting truck, and the driver started the motor. Behind them they were leaving their home, their possessions, and many memories. The last thing they saw was Katsy's mother, waving a handkerchief as she stood by the gate.

6

NIGHTMARE
VOYAGE

LATER THE SAME DAY THEY ARRIVED AT ONE OF THE damaged piers in Manila harbor, and were placed on a hospital ship already crowded with wounded Japanese soldiers. Their fellow evacuees also came aboard: eight men and women returning to their homes in Central and South America.

The voyage to Formosa was to last five days. It soon became a nightmare. The evacuees were not allowed a moment's privacy. Guards were assigned to watch them at all times. Still worse, there were no drugs on the ship, and the screams of the wounded kept everyone's nerves on edge.

But for Chick Parsons, there was something far more harrowing to think about. On the first evening they had crowded wearily into their one small cabin, where the boys finally had fallen asleep. Their Japanese guard sat dozing in the open doorway. A badly wounded soldier moaned somewhere in the bowels of the ship. Since they had come aboard, Parsons and his wife had not been alone for a second. Now, in the dark, she told him something that almost made his hair stand on end.

"I packed the intelligence file yesterday," she whispered. "At first I thought it might be better not to bring it, but I couldn't be sure. And later, after Mother said she wasn't coming, well, there just never seemed to be any time to ask you about it."

"You mean we've got that stuff on the ship with us? The newspapers? The prisoners' names? Everything?"

"I'm afraid so."

"Where did you pack it?"

"In the suitcase. Under the baby's diapers."

Parsons closed his eyes, and drew a long breath. After a moment he said, "If we tried to take that file through Customs, they'd catch us for sure. We've got to get rid of every last scrap before we reach Formosa."

"Do you think we'll have any trouble doing it?" she asked him. "The first time one of the guards isn't looking, why can't we just flush all the papers down the toilet?"

"That might work," he said. And he tried not to think of what the secret police agent had told him the last night in Santo Tomás: *A person caught trying to smuggle such things through Customs would be executed on the spot.*

For the rest of the voyage he and Katsy watched for a chance to dispose of the incriminating papers. But the chance never seemed to come. A guard was always close by, only a few feet away, ready to give the alarm if anyone made a suspicious move. It was impossible to escape surveillance, even by going to the washroom. The guard went right in with you—and a nurse went in with the women and children.

All during the next four days and nights, Parsons tried to work out a scheme for destroying the file. Each plan, he knew, was doomed to fail. The Japanese did not relax their vigilance. At any given moment he could look across the deck and see one of the guards, still on the alert, eyeing him coldly. Meanwhile, the suitcase remained in the cabin, tucked neatly away under the bed. Inside was the file, a little collection of information that would become his death warrant in a few hours more.

When their ship finally reached Takao, in Formosa, the evacuees found themselves herded into a metal-sided truck. Their baggage was hurled in after them, and the door locked. After a short, jolting ride, the truck stopped. A Japanese Customs official, unquestionably a member of the Kempeitai, unlocked the door. Looking out the back, Parsons could see that their party had been driven to a long, open shed.

"Inspection!" the Customs man shouted. "Each person stand by own luggage!"

Parsons looked down at the small suitcase. The situation seemed hopeless. The place was alive with Customs inspectors. In a few minutes one of them was bound to find the papers. After that, if he was extremely fortunate, a soldier would lead him around the corner and shoot him at once.

Inside the shed, he and Katsy took their place at the back of the line. The trunk was beside them, and the small suitcase. Under his arm he held a leather briefcase. It contained the identification papers of his own family and those of their eight fellow evacuees.

At the head of the line, the first two couples were in the process of having their baggage checked. The inspectors were being very thorough. They dumped out the contents of each bag and trunk, held up an item, ran their nimble fingers along the seams, into the corners, patting, testing, surveying the most innocent-looking box or garment with intense suspicion. They seemed to miss nothing. It would take them about three seconds to spot the intelligence file, pounce on it, and start asking angry questions to which there could be no satisfactory reply. . . .

He felt a gentle tug at one of his trouser legs. Glancing down, he saw it was Pete, their four-year-old. Not knowing what was happening, the boy still must have sensed that something was wrong. A worried expression said that, whatever was troubling his father, he wanted to help.

Parsons looked around. Across the way was a huge pillar, supporting the roof of the shed. Suddenly, the beginning of a plan began to form in his mind. He knelt down, and said in a calm voice, "You see this bag, Pete?" He patted the small suitcase. "I want you to pick it up, and then walk very quietly over to that big post. After that, put the bag down, and sit on it. And don't move again until I tell you."

The little boy nodded, picked up the bag with both

hands, and tottered away. He put it down by the post. Then he sat on it, and looked around, to see what was going to happen next.

To Parsons' dismay, a pair of guards immediately came up and began to talk to Pete. Both of the older Parsons children had learned a considerable amount of Japanese slang since the enemy soldiers had come to Manila. Now Pete turned a questioning glance at his father. Should he talk to these strangers? Parsons nodded imperceptibly, and Pete began to chatter away at the guards. The soldiers were delighted to find a Western child who could speak Japanese. They reached into their knapsacks, and took out fruit and candy. They pressed their gifts into Pete's small hands.

"Parsons!" a sharp voice cried. "Two piece luggage! Open trunk first!"

Everything in their trunk was dumped out on the dirty floor of the shed, and examined closely. Then the contents were thrust back inside, and the lid slammed shut. One inspector scribbled something in chalk on the side. Another said, "Second piece luggage!"

It was now or never. He raised the leather briefcase and held it out to the inspector.

The Customs man looked, and then dropped his eyes to the paper he was holding. "List say *suitcase,*" he announced suspiciously.

"Mistake," Parsons said, bowing politely to express his apologies. "*Small* suitcase." He tapped it softly. "*Brief*case."

The inspector hesitated. He consulted the paper several times. Finally he shrugged. He opened the case and examined the identification papers of the party. Then he shut the case. A few chalk marks went on the side.

The chief inspector shouted, "Return luggage and persons to truck immediately!"

Parsons felt his hands grow cold with sweat. Although they were "through" Customs now, he still had to do something about the uninspected suitcase. He couldn't just leave it behind in the shed. But if he walked across and picked it up himself, in order to carry it over to the truck, the inspector at his elbow was almost sure to see him do so. And the inspector would wonder why the Panamanian Consul had a briefcase *and* a suitcase now—a suitcase with no chalk marks on the side, showing that it had not been examined.

There was only one thing to do, one possible way to slip the bag into the truck without the inspector noticing it. Parsons looked over at his son. "Bring the bag, Pete," he called out softly. "And come on back to the truck."

Pete got up and started. But the soldiers had been too generous. They had given him so much fruit and candy that his pockets couldn't hold everything. As he tried to pick up the bag, some of the candy and fruit spilled on the floor. Chocolate bars cascaded down; grapes rolled around the pillar.

The soldiers saw Pete's difficulties, and broke into roars of laughter. Then they hurried over and took charge. They picked up the fallen candy, the fruit, the suitcase, and Pete along with the rest. In one swoop all were carried across the shed, past the Customs inspectors, and then were placed inside the waiting truck.

Just as the motor was starting, one of the soldiers pointed a warning finger at Pete. He shouted something in Japanese, as the truck rolled away.

"What was he saying?" Chick asked Katsy.

"He told Pete the next time he went on a trip, he shouldn't try to take so much along. He said it's better to travel light."

Parsons nodded. Under his breath he said a very quiet, "Amen."

Once their luggage had passed through Customs at Takao, Parsons felt sure that it would not be reexamined, and so he decided to run the minor risk of keeping the intelligence file. As things turned out, his guess was right; the suitcase and trunk were not inspected again. But before they left Formosa, there were other anxious moments. At Takao, the evacuees were placed in a brand-new prisoner of war encampment. They were its only inhabitants. From morning till night they had nothing to do but eat and sleep.

After a day or two, Mike Parsons and his younger brother Pete began to feel bored with prison life. Beyond the barbed wire fence there were city streets, bustling with activity. So, they waited till no one was looking, and crawled under the fence.

Two young guards spied them and brought them back. The next day the boys slipped away again. The young guards returned them, and then, painfully thumbing through a Japanese-English dictionary, asked Chick and Katsy Parsons to "please stop your children from escaping."

On the day the evacuees were to leave Takao, Mike

Parsons disappeared a third time. The frantic guards rushed out to search for him. He was nowhere to be found.

A half hour passed. It looked as though the Parsons family would have to be left behind. But at the last moment the guards reappeared, smiling with relief. While they had been hunting everywhere for him, Mike had been sitting just around the corner—watching an inning or two of a local baseball game.

Chick and Katsy were still recovering from this experience when the entire party was ordered back into a truck. They left the camp, and after a short ride found themselves at the airport. Ahead lay the flight to Shanghai, and then the long sea voyage that finally would bring them to safety in America.

At the airport they passed from the hands of the secret police to military control. The atmosphere immediately became more friendly. The guards relaxed as soon as the last Kempeitai agent disappeared, and the air-force commandant invited the evacuees into his spacious offices. Candy was found for Mike and Pete, and a couch for Patrick to have a nap on. Before long, the plane could be heard outside, warming up. The commandant rose and led them to the runway.

Parsons looked at their plane, and said without thinking, "Why, it's a Douglas." The moment he'd said it, he knew it was a blunder.

The commandant's smile faded. He bristled with suspicion. "The Consul for Panama has had occasion to ride on American planes?"

"Now and then," Parsons said casually. "Of course."

"And under what circumstances? From where to where?"

"Manila to Baguio, the summer capital. To escape the heat."

The answers had come out so easily that the commandant's doubts were allayed. He began to smile cordially again, and after a moment or two, saw a chance to spread some propaganda. He said to Parsons, "Surely, then, the Honorable Consul will not object to flying to Shanghai in this inferior machine—abandoned by the cowardly Americans when they fled before the victorious forces of the emperor?"

"It will be a real delight," Parsons said.

The commandant bowed. Parsons returned the bow. "And please remember," the commandant added, "to tell your people at home the truth about Japanese hospitality."

"Believe me, I'll certainly do that, *amigo,*" Parsons said.

The flight from Formosa was uneventful. They stayed in Shanghai for a week or two, enjoying good food, hot baths, and rest. Then they boarded a passenger ship, the *Conte Verde,* sailing first to Singapore and afterward to a port in Portuguese South Africa where, after being exchanged for Japanese civilians, they boarded a second ship, the *Gripsholm,* and the Swedish vessel carried them to Rio de Janiero.

On August 29, 1942, Chick Parsons arrived in New York with Katsy and their three boys, and learned that since the fall of Manila he had been listed as "Missing in Action." Now, waiting officials told him that he had been promoted to lieutenant commander and that he was entitled to take leave, before returning to duty. In a hotel room they listened to an account of his experiences, and then asked him about the intelligence file he and Katsy had brought out with so much difficulty.

Parsons found a house for his family in North Carolina, and then visited his father and mother in Tennessee. Several weeks later he returned to duty in Washington. He had not been there too long, when a sealed message arrived at his desk.

It was from a Colonel Evans, in the Intelligence Section of Army G-2. The colonel wanted very much to see Commander Parsons. The subject was classified and quite urgent. Would Parsons get in touch with him as quickly as possible?

They made an appointment for the same afternoon. Still, Parsons thought the whole thing puzzling. What could Army Intelligence want with him? And why were they in such a hurry to have him come over?

He had other questions on his mind, too. What sort of assignment should he put in for next? He had already experienced enough danger to last a lifetime; he had already taken more risks than most men did during an entire war. Perhaps the best idea would be to stay in the capital, and enjoy the easy life for a while.

Parsons grinned to himself. He knew he wouldn't remain happy for very long with a Washington desk job. No, he'd better request something a little more active, something that might even hold a few risks.

He put on his cap, and walked out into the pale autumn sunlight. *Colonel Evans, Army Intelligence.* Now, what in the world could a G-2 colonel want to see him about?

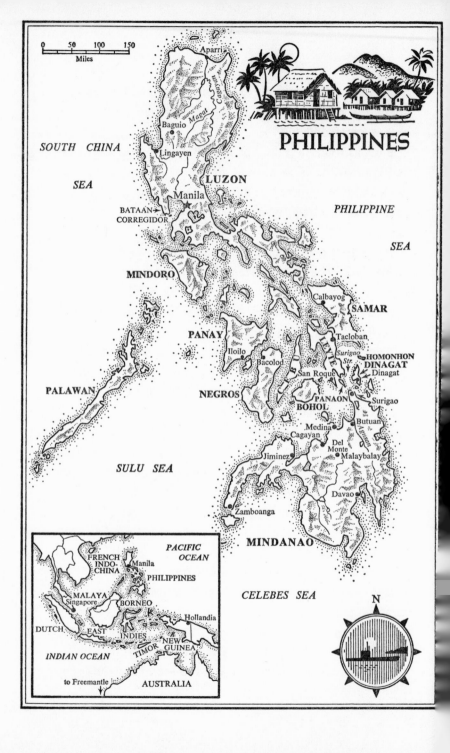

7

SEND
PARSONS

COLONEL EVANS HAD A STORY TO TELL. A FEW DAYS before, in early October, 1942, the powerful Mackay monitoring station in San Francisco had been beamed toward the Philippines. Weak but persistent signals had been picked up from a shortwave transmitter on Panay, the sixth largest of the Islands.

In all, several messages had been received from the Panay station. The sender identified himself as Macario Peralta, a major in the Philippine Army. He said that he had gathered a band of men in the hills. They were armed and well organized. They had attacked Japanese forces on the island several times, and would continue to do so as long as their ammunition lasted. His men were fighting, the major said, to restore their country's freedom. Would

America answer? Would she send the "aid" promised to the Philippine people so many months ago?

The possibility that guerrilla fighters might be at work in the Islands, the colonel said, was of great interest to Washington and to General MacArthur in Australia. But of course, before the United States Government could take any action, certain questions would have to be decided. For one thing, were the messages what they seemed to be? Or were they merely a Japanese trick, designed to lure American men and supplies to Panay, where they could be destroyed or captured?

"We know you've just escaped from the Islands," the colonel told Parsons, "so we figured you'd probably have a pretty good idea of the situation back there. How do you size up this Major Peralta? Does his story ring true—or do you think it's a trap?"

Parsons studied the sheaf of messages that Colonel Evans had placed before him on the desk. After considering them carefully, he said: "Naturally, I can't be sure. But my guess would be that Major Peralta and his men are the real thing."

"And what about the rest of the Islands?" the colonel asked. "Might some other guerrillas be operating there— groups we ought to be trying to supply with ammunition and equipment?"

"I just don't know," Parsons said. "Before I left, there certainly was no organized movement on Luzon. I found quite a number of armed men outside Manila, but they weren't acting together; they hadn't formed an effective force; it was still everyone for himself.

"On the other hand, we did hear rumors about the central and southern islands. A large number of officers and men were said to have taken to the backcountry, on Mindanao, Samar, Leyte, Panay—and apparently some of them were talking about moving into action against the Japanese. I'm sure the potential's there for a guerrilla movement. But whether or not more than a handful of men have gone beyond the talking stage, I just wouldn't know."

"Fair enough," the colonel said with a sigh. "But it still leave us pretty much in the dark. Not just about this Major Peralta on Panay, but about the rest of the Islands, too. We badly need firsthand information on what's happening there. Only, for the life of me, I can't see how we're going to get it."

"Unless," Parsons said, "you send somebody in to have a look around."

Colonel Evans glanced at him sharply. "Send an agent in blind? That could be a very rough assignment."

"I'm not sure it would have to be all that rough," Parsons said. "Not if your agent really was familiar with the country. You need someone who's lived in the Islands a good part of his life, a man who knows some of the local dialects, and who could, in a pinch, pass himself off as one of the natives."

"It sounds like you might be trying to talk yourself into a job, Commander." The colonel paused. "Are you?"

Parsons thought the matter over. Finally he said, "I guess that *is* about the size of it."

"Nobody would think of asking you to go back in," the colonel told him, "not after what you've already been through. And don't forget, the Nips must know who you really are by now. They'd be very happy to get their hands on you again."

"I wouldn't go back with the idea of letting them," Parsons said. "Besides, the assignment would take care of one of my problems. The last couple of days I've been feeling sort of restless, here in Washington. Stateside life doesn't seem to agree with me. What do you think, Colonel? Could the army and navy get together on this?"

The colonel nodded. "G-2 will be glad to work with your Naval Intelligence boys. Draft us a memorandum, first. Put down a few ideas. Tell us what you believe you might be able to do in the Islands, if someone can put you back in there." The colonel gathered up the sheaf of radio messages, and prepared to return them to his safe. "Then I'll see what can be done about getting the project started."

For the next few days, Parsons worked on a tentative plan for Army and Navy Intelligence. After several conferences the plan was agreed to, and then sent up through channels. Toward the end of the year, it reached General MacArthur's headquarters in Australia.

A reply wasn't long in coming. In Washington, the Navy Department received a telegram: SEND PARSONS IMMEDIATELY. It was signed: MACARTHUR.

A few hours later, Parsons had packed a small handbag, phoned goodbye to his family and was heading back to the Southwest Pacific.

When he arrived in Australia, Chick Parsons found that the prospects for an organized guerrilla campaign in the

Islands seemed much brighter than anyone had believed possible even a few weeks earlier. An increasing number of shortwave radio messages were being received almost daily. The senders said they were Philippine soldiers, anxious to get in touch with the commanding general of the Southwest Pacific Theater. They wanted to set up regular communications channels, and hoped that eventually General MacArthur would send them the promised "aid."

In addition, Parsons learned, several American and Filipino servicemen had managed to escape to the south from enemy-held territory. Thanks to the stories these escapees told, it was possible now to form a reasonably accurate picture of recent events in the central and southern islands. The picture contained many hopeful signs.

Of primary importance was the fact that during the early months of the war, while Bataan and Corregidor had been besieged, the central and southern islands had remained relatively free of Japanese forces. The Americans on Leyte, Mindanao, Samar and other islands, under General William F. Sharp, had realized their comrades on Luzon could not continue to resist indefinitely. Nevertheless, even if Bataan and Corregidor were to fall, they themselves hoped to conduct a broad holding operation in the remainder of the Territory. Eventually, they reasoned, reinforcements and supplies would reach them from America, and then they could attack the Japanese in a renewal of the full-scale, open warfare for which they'd been trained.

To further the scheme, many local Filipinos were added to the ranks. These volunteers were mostly young men between seventeen and twenty-four, fit, active, and eager to engage the enemy. Within a short time they were given at least part of an intensive course of military instruction. During the same period, supplies of food and ammunition were removed from nearby warehouses, and carried away to hiding places in the mountains.

Although the plan was ready, it was never carried out. The capitulation of Corregidor changed everything; the Japanese threatened to kill the fortress's twelve thousand defenders if General Sharp refused to surrender his troops in the south, and the general and his staff decided they had no choice but to comply.

For one thing, the enemy was perfectly capable of carrying out the promised massacre. For another, there was the recent discovery that no assistance from America was likely to arrive for months or even years. What was to be gained, then, by holding out in the rest of the Territory? Unable to live off the countryside, and lacking new supplies and reinforcements, American soldiers soon would be at the enemy's mercy. Further fighting, it was agreed, would lead only to needless bloodshed and suffering; shortly after Corregidor's fall, the remaining United States units throughout the Islands gave up their arms.

But the recently trained Filipino recruits were not included in the surrender terms—or at least no one in the south seemed to feel they were. Farmers, clerks, businessmen, they saw no point in marching docilely into prison camp along with the Americans. Instead, they decided to put away their rifles and ammunition, and return to civilian life.

In many instances, American officers helped them to

avoid imprisonment by deliberately omitting their names from the official rosters handed over to Japanese authorities. Undetected, thousands of Filipino volunteers went back home, buried their arms, and took up their former occupations. Then they settled down to await the day when General MacArthur would return.

During June, July, and August, 1942, the Japanese occupied the central and southern islands. At first, they did not come in large numbers. They established garrisons of about a hundred men in the major cities, and outposts of only six or eight men in the smaller towns. Much of the countryside, particularly the mountains and the farming areas, saw almost nothing of the invaders, except, perhaps, for a very rare patrol.

On most of the islands there was no local police force now. The old Philippine Constabulary had been a part of the army; following their arrival in the south, the Japanese had disbanded the organization. With nothing to hold them in check, lawless elements in the population soon began to stir. It wasn't long before gangs of marauders were setting out from the cities to loot the countryside. Brandishing a few weapons, they forced the helpless villagers and farmers to hand over money, tools, clothing, and livestock.

But after being pillaged once or twice, many former recruits decided they'd had enough. They dug up their guns, banded together, and drove the brigands out of their neighborhoods. As a matter of security, these vigilante groups began to form larger units, to protect a greater amount of territory. The brigands saw they had met their match, and their incursions into the countryside came to an abrupt end.

But the bands of ex-soldiers remained in the field. They were young; they had received a few weeks' military training; and they possessed a considerable number of weapons. They were a potential guerrilla force, needing only competent leaders to forge them into effective underground battalions.

Such leadership was close at hand. In almost every rural district there were American and Filipino officers who had chosen to go into hiding rather than surrender to the Japanese. Many were professional soldiers. In numerous instances they were the very officers who had trained the district's youthful volunteers, before the fall of Corregidor.

These young volunteers remembered them, and respected their military experience. It made no difference that now the officers might be wearing tattered uniforms or that their gold or silver bars might be tarnished. They were invited to take command, and almost simultaneously, throughout the central and southern islands, a native guerrilla movement sprang into being.

These were the diverse and scattered groups, Chick Parsons realized, that had to be organized into a single cohesive force. The task would not be easy. The size of the guerrilla bands, their location, reliability, and leadership were only vaguely known. Yet these uncertainties were inconsequential. Only one thing mattered: Back in the Islands, many ordinary Filipinos were ready to risk their lives fighting the invaders. A vision of freedom still flourished there, and it was this that made his imminent return seem even more important than it had a few weeks before.

8

THE
ODYSSEY BEGINS

EARLY IN 1943, WITH THE FULL APPROVAL OF GENERAL MacArthur, a small top-secret project was authorized in Australia. In time, it came to be known as "Spyron," a term derived from the words "spy squadron." Initially, the project's personnel consisted of one man—Lieutenant Commander Charles Parsons.

Having been relieved of regular naval duties, Parsons found himself free to roll up his sleeves and set to work. After consulting with Army, Navy, and Air Force staff officers, he began to draw up a list of the things that headquarters hoped he could accomplish on his return to the Islands.

First, it was essential for him to learn the extent of the

guerrilla movement, the ability and trustworthiness of different leaders, and the amount of arms and equipment they already possessed. Those leaders who appeared capable, and who were willing to accept orders from General MacArthur, were to receive official recognition. They would be assured of future supplies, and their groups would become a part of the intelligence organization the general wished to see introduced into the Philippines.

While traveling about, Parsons would bring token supplies to those guerrilla groups that received official recognition. At selected sites he would establish "coast-watcher" stations to gather information on Japanese shipping. Finally, he would attempt to encourage the Philippine people to begin to make an effective resistance against the enemy. As he confessed to one of his fellow officers, "It's quite an ambitious plan."

There were those at Headquarters who didn't give him much chance of success. They were certain that any American foolhardy enough to enter enemy-held territory would soon be discovered, tracked down, and put to death.

Parsons disagreed. He knew the people well, and was familiar with their ways. He trusted them, and believed that a large majority could be counted on to help. He wouldn't find the language a great problem, either. He was fluent in Spanish, and could get by in a couple of local dialects. And his appearance would be an asset. He was short—like the average Filipino—and dark, so that at a distance, except for his rather broad shoulders, he could easily pass for a native.

"But suppose one day you should run smack into some

Nips?" he was asked. "What'll you do then—try to shoot your way out?"

"I don't intend to run into them," Parsons said. "I'm going back as a spy, not a commando. As far as I'm concerned, there won't *be* any shooting—I don't even plan to carry a gun."

Almost every day, it seemed, a new problem arose. There was the question of transportation. The only way to reach the Philippines was by submarine, but at first the Navy was reluctant to allow one of its few U-boats to be diverted from regular duty. Parsons argued patiently that a submarine would lose little time on a Spyron mission, and that eventually the Navy stood to gain a great deal from the coast-watcher stations he proposed to establish. After long discussions with his superiors, he finally was granted permission to "hitch a ride" on one of the regular fleet submarines.

The selection and packing of the expedition's equipment required both sound judgment and ingenuity. Spyron was allotted all the extra space aboard one of the subs in port, but after the usual supplies of food, ammunition, and torpedoes had been stowed away, it was found that there wasn't much "extra" space aboard. Parsons decided to give top priority to radio equipment; he included a few large sets, which the guerrillas would need to reach Australia, and some smaller ones for their local communications. He also packed away batteries, generators, and spare parts.

Medicine came next, especially a quantity of atabrine, for use against malaria. Then arms, ammunition, and Quartermaster clothing and food were squeezed in, and finally a fifty-pound can of wheat flour, to enable the people, who were 95 percent Catholic, to make Communion wafers.

One of the last things to be determined was the place where he would land. The decision was still being debated when Captain Charles Smith, a laconic young army officer, arrived at Fremantle, Australia. A few days earlier, Smith and two companions had been picked up off the coast in a small open boat. They had sailed to Australia from the Philippines to inform General MacArthur of an important guerrilla band, then being formed in southern Mindanao, by an American officer named Wendell Fertig.

According to Smith, Colonel Fertig's troops were numerous, armed, and well disciplined. They controlled much of the local country, outside the towns. Parsons decided to land in southern Mindanao and get in touch with Colonel Fertig. After that, he would proceed north to some of the other islands by whatever means of transportation seemed most suitable. Captain Smith also fitted into his plans. He invited the young officer to become a member of the expedition, and Smith quickly agreed.

By now it was February, 1943, and there was very little time left before their departure. They finished stowing away their equipment in the forward and aft torpedo rooms; soon they were joined by the rest of their party: two Moros from southern Mindanao, in native costume, whose knowledge of the local terrain was considered likely to be of value.

The crew cast off, the motors turned, and the slim, cigar-shaped vessel edged away from the dock at Fremantle. Ahead, the antisubmarine nets parted. The ship sailed past, and the nets closed again over their wake. The first install-

ment of the "aid," promised so long ago, finally was on its
way to the Philippine people.

The submarine glided northward, through the Celebes
Sea, toward the wild and remote site on the southern coast
of Mindanao selected for their initial landing. On the way,
ordinary duties were carried out. Several torpedoes were
launched against Japanese ships, and more than once the
sub was forced to crash dive, in order to escape answering
depth charges. Luckily, no damage was received. The
explosions merely rattled their steel plates for a few moments, and then, the encounter over, the ship's diesels came
reassuringly back to life again.

As the voyage drew to an end, Parsons reviewed last-
minute details. He and the two Moros would leave the submarine in a small boat, under cover of darkness. He would
be dressed simply. Headquarters had urged him to adopt a
disguise, but his instincts told him that such a plan would be
a mistake. He wished the Filipinos to see him for what he
was—an American officer bringing the first token aid from
General MacArthur—and he feared that any disguise could
all too easily create doubt and confusion, and perhaps add
needlessly to the risk.

Once ashore, he planned to reach whatever guerrilla
forces might be in the area. Presumably, they would be
some of Colonel Fertig's men. If this proved to be so, and if
the overall situation appeared satisfactory, small fishing
boats, called *vintas,* would be sent out from shore within a
short time. The vintas would be flying previously agreed-on
signals to indicate that all was well. They would proceed to

the waiting submarine, to unload the supplies from Spyron.

If the vintas did not appear as arranged, it would indicate that Parsons had met trouble. In that case, he was to be considered on his own. No attempt would be made to rescue him. The submarine would continue with its mission, and, later, Captain Smith would try to effect a new landing, at a second site previously selected.

One evening, in March, the submarine arrived off the coast of Mindanao. It was already midnight. The skipper brought them to within a few feet of the surface. Through the periscope he surveyed the surrounding waters and the dark outline of the distant shore. Everything seemed quiet. He gave a command, and the submarine rose till its streaming decks had cleared the water. A hatch opened. Parsons shook hands with Charley Smith. Then, one by one, he and his Moro companions followed two of the ship's officers up the hatch.

A small rubber boat was inflated and put over the side. The Moros climbed in and took up their oars. They were naked to the waist. In their belts they had hung their bolos, the long, sharp knives the natives of Mindanao used so efficiently.

Parsons climbed in and found a seat between the two oarsmen. He was dressed in an old bleached khaki shirt and a pair of shorts. He was barefoot. Around his neck hung a pair of canvas sandals.

The ship's officers handed him a waterproof knapsack. He raised his hand, making a circle with thumb and forefinger—the American serviceman's traditional gesture of approval or way of saying "Good luck!" The Moros began to paddle, and the round, clumsy boat soon drew away. Behind them, the submarine quietly submerged, disturbing the dark surface of the water with a momentary surge of white foam. Then the turmoil subsided, and the small rubber boat was alone.

The Moros thrust in their oars, and they began to move with painful slowness toward the distant crescent of the lagoon. The morning winds were already rising. Small whitecaps slapped at the sides of the boat. The tide was running out strongly, and the Moros grunted as they labored against it. There was no moon, but the sky had brightened perceptibly by the time a break appeared in the reef.

Dawn was coming much too quickly. Parsons could make out individual palm trees on the shore, and beneath them, a white strip of sandy beach. The submarine must have left them off too far away. At all costs they had to be safely ashore and hidden in the underbrush before daybreak.

"*Pas, pas,*" he murmured to the Moros. "Faster, faster . . ." They dug in their oars, and finally the boat slipped past the narrow break in the reef, into the calm waters of the lagoon.

It was light now, but they were drawing near shore. In another few minutes they would be on land again, ready to fade into the countryside. . . .

A hail of bullets struck the water. With a sigh, they ricocheted into the distance.

"Japanese!" the Moros whispered. They sat frozen, their

paddles raised. They looked at Parsons with huge, terrified eyes. They were jungle fighters, and the water was not their natural element.

"Too late to turn," Parsons told them. "We must keep going in."

The Moros began to row again. Another volley struck the water. The firing was more scattered, though, as if the marksmen on shore were growing uncertain. They could be seen now, slipping from tree to tree, keeping cover, and apparently talking among themselves.

Parsons still couldn't make out their uniforms. Maybe the marksmen were Japanese, or perhaps Filipinos who thought that he and the Moros were a small enemy landing party, and were greeting them accordingly. At least they had stopped firing. The Moros rowed steadily, and at last the rubber boat slid up on the sand.

There was no sign of life when Parsons climbed out and began to walk toward the underbrush. He did not carry a weapon. If the men were Filipinos, he wouldn't need side-arms, and if they were Japanese a rifle or a pistol would be of far less use than a good story, to cover their arrival on that remote stretch of southern beach. . . .

An armed man stepped out from behind a tree. He was wearing the peaked cap of a Japanese soldier. His ragged shirt and shorts were also Japanese. *But, thank God, he wore no shoes.* The Japanese never went barefoot. The man was a Filipino.

"Hello," Parsons shouted.

"Who are you?" The guerrilla gave his rifle a small flourish.

"I'm a messenger from General Douglas MacArthur. I bring you greetings and supplies from his headquarters in Australia." He turned halfway round, and pointed to the boat.

Other men rose from the underbrush to join their leader on the edge of the beach. They watched Parsons in silence as he opened the waterproof knapsack. At first, they didn't understand what he was doing when he offered them American cigarettes, candy bars, chewing gum. Then, as they recognized the well-remembered objects in his hands, they began to shout. Dozens of other ragged men came out of hiding and hurried down to the shore. They swarmed around him, accepted the gifts, hugged him, and all the while chattered away, their eyes bright with emotion.

Soon their wives and children came, and even the sick and the elderly left their fires in the village and hobbled down to the beach.

By now the sun was up, over the blue waters of the lagoon. Parsons looked around him. The tough guerrilla fighters were squatting in the sand, and, to his amazement, he saw that tears of joy were streaming down their hard, leathery cheeks.

9

MINDANAO

THE REST OF THE LANDING OPERATION WAS SOON UNDER-
way. A small fleet of vintas left its hidden anchorage in a
nearby river, sailed out to meet the submarine, and began
to unload the expedition's supplies.

As he waited on shore, Parsons noticed a stir in the
crowd. An old woman from the village seemed to be staring
at him. Suddenly she screamed, "It's Chico!" and, rushing
up, happily threw her arms around him.

She was a *lavandera,* a washerwoman, who had worked
for Katsy and her family in Zamboanga many years ago. He
remembered that she had always been a great favorite of
the Jurikas. Now she chattered away at a great rate,
scarcely giving him a chance to tell her about Blanche and

Tommy Jurika, and about Katsy and their own three boys.

But even as she talked, he felt a momentary chill. For here he was, on the beach less than an hour, and already an old friend had broadcast his identity to everyone within earshot. If he had been using a cover story, pretending to be anyone but an American named Chick Parsons, the encounter would have created confusion in the minds of the "trigger-happy" guerrillas crowding around them. The incident confirmed his feeling that it would always be a wise policy to play things straight, and not attempt to pose as someone else.

When the supplies had been brought ashore, Parsons, Charley Smith, the guerrilla soldiers, and some of the villagers faded away as quickly as possible into the countryside. Later, they learned that they had not moved any too quickly. The submarine had been observed by native agents of the Japanese. Several of them had sped off to the town of Cagayan, a hundred miles away, to alert the enemy garrison.

Because the agents wanted to make their information sound important, they reported that six large cargo-carrying submarines had landed tons of supplies and hundreds of men on the beach. The next day a strong enemy patrol rushed up from Cagayan. The Japanese found nothing but a few dead fires and some American cigarettes, smoked down to the very end. By then, Parsons and his party were far back in the hills, approaching the headquarters of Colonel Fertig.

A native of West Virginia, and a mining engineer by profession, the colonel, like many American residents in the

Philippines, had held a reserve commission prior to the war. After Pearl Harbor he had been ordered to Bataan, and had served there until the fall of the peninsula. Then he had escaped by plane to Mindanao, where he had helped train young Filipino recruits. Following the final surrender in the south, he had taken to the backcountry to avoid imprisonment. A number of officers and enlisted men had decided to accompany him; they now formed the cadre of Fertig's widespread guerrilla movement.

From the start, the colonel made a favorable impression on Parsons. The morale of his soldiers appeared to be high. He himself seemed to be a man of calm judgment and intelligence, the sort of leader General MacArthur had hoped might be present in the Philippines.

Still, it paid to be sure. One night, after supper, Parsons had a chance to talk with his host.

"How many rifles do you have?" Parsons asked. "Five hundred?"

"Five thousand would be closer," the colonel told him.

Parsons let out a whistle. "We had no idea it was anywhere near that many. What ratio of rifles to men?"

"About one to three."

"How have you set up your organization?"

"Into districts around the island," the colonel said. "My staff officers are out in the field."

"Which is where they ought to be. Who are some of them?"

"MacLish, Bowler, Hedges . . ."

Parsons nodded. Before the war he had known the three quite well in Manila. They were American businessmen with reserve commissions, an excellent trio of officers for any guerrilla organization. Surely, things on Mindanao were in better shape than G-2 or Naval Intelligence had guessed.

Colonel Fertig made it clear, though, while describing the general situation on the island, that conditions varied widely from district to district. One bright spot was in the south, where Hedges was doing a fine job with the fierce Moro tribesmen. Another was up the coast to the north, where MacLish had a seasoned group of guerrillas under tight control. The east appeared reasonably well taken care of by Bowler, but it was hard to be absolutely sure. The island was so large, the few roads so poor, and the intervening mountains and jungles so difficult to cross, that communications between the colonel and his staff officer in the east were almost nonexistent. It took three weeks to send a message overland from western to eastern Mindanao, and of course that meant six weeks elapsed before a reply was received.

There were other difficulties, too. A number of guerrilla bands were scattered about the island. Most were quite small; all insisted on maintaining their independence. The worst situation existed in the Del Monte region, where a man named Salipada Pendatun had gathered together a powerful and potentially useful force of ex-soldiers, Moros, and young recruits. Unfortunately, "Brigadier General" Pendatun, as he titled himself, refused to cooperate in any way whatever. It reduced the effectiveness of both organizations, the colonel said, but to date he hadn't been able to do much to improve matters.

When his host had finished, Parsons considered all that he had been told. Then he said: "I think several things ought to be done, here on Mindanao. First, your different groups must have more arms and ammunition. Second, they should have enough radio equipment to communicate with you, with Australia, and with one another. And third, as soon as possible, all the guerrilla forces on the island should be brought into a single organization. They must recognize one leader, who will take his orders, through me, from General MacArthur. Does that sound like a workable plan?"

"It does," the colonel said.

"Fine. Then as soon as I've had a chance to look at more of Mindanao, to set up the first coast-watcher stations, and perhaps to visit some of the other islands, I'll go back to Australia and ask them to start shipping you all the arms, ammunition, and other supplies you need. In the meantime, you can start setting up two of the radios we've brought in. And while I'm still here, I'll also see what I can do to persuade this 'Brigadier General' Pendatun to join your organization. I don't think I'll have much trouble, once your command has been formally recognized."

"*My* command?"

"Of course. From what Charley Smith told us about you, General MacArthur was pretty sure you were the right man to run things here on Mindanao. And now, from what I've seen myself and from what you've told me, I'm convinced of it. As soon as I can, I'll get in touch with Australia, and by the end of the week your appointment as leader of the Tenth Military District of Mindanao should be confirmed. While you're waiting, though, you might like to wear these."

Parsons drew a pair of silver eagles from his pocket, and handed them to Colonel Fertig. "You're in the army again—or should I say 'still'?"

The colonel pinned on the new insignia. "I'll do my best," he said softly.

"We know you will," Parsons said. "And now that we've got you back in—here's the general's first order. After this, there'll be no more open warfare against the Japanese. Harass the enemy as much as you please, ambush his patrols, observe and report every move he makes on sea or land, but never fight him in the open or attack when he's in garrison. You can't win with rifles against what he's got. You'll only bring reprisals and suffering to the people. Someday, when Spyron's brought you the arms you need, and when American troops land in the Islands, it will be a different story. Would you agree that the general's order seems reasonable, Colonel?"

"Perfectly reasonable to me," Fertig said.

"Then I think we can say officially that things are beginning to look pretty good on Mindanao."

During the next phase of his mission, Chick Parsons found himself back in familiar territory. He first had seen the southern and central islands more than twenty years ago, when he had sailed as a young man aboard General Leonard Wood's yacht, the *Apo*. This time his ship was the

Narra Maru, a sixty-foot Japanese diesel launch, recently captured from the enemy by Colonel Fertig's guerrillas.

Parsons was extremely pleased when the ship was put at his disposal. It was a long way to Surigao Strait, where he planned to set up a coast-watcher radio station. By using the ship, he could avoid many weary days of tramping through Mindanao's tangled jungle thickets and along the island's winding mountain trails.

Travel by sea was comparatively swift and comfortable, but it was not without danger. The launch carried enemy markings; a Japanese flag fluttered at the masthead; and there was another Rising Sun painted on the deck. None of these would do much good, however, if they met a well-armed enemy patrol boat. Unable to respond to her signals, their ruse would quickly be discovered, and a boarding party would put an end to Spyron's designs. To avoid such an encounter, the *Narra Maru* sailed only at night, staying as close to shore as the helmsman dared.

Eventually they reached the town of Medina, on the north coast, where Lieutenant Colonel Ernest MacLish had established his headquarters. Parsons was pleased to find enthusiasm high in the colonel's territory, and to learn that his men had overcome a variety of shortages with typical guerrilla ingenuity.

As an example, when the colonel's men serviced the *Narra Maru,* shortly after the ship had tied up at the dock, they did not pump in diesel fuel, for none was available in the area. Instead, they began to fill the ship's tanks with coconut oil, which they had produced themselves from almost unlimited supplies of coconuts. It was a fine substitute, the colonel assured Parsons. It was clean-starting, clean-burning, and totally satisfactory for running a diesel launch.

"The coconut palm," MacLish went on, "is vital to us here. My men use one part of the tree for food, and another part to make some of their clothing. And as I've already said, you can run a diesel motor perfectly well on coconut oil. It's true that for gasoline motors you do need another kind of alcohol—but you can distill it from the juice of the palm flower, which the natives around here call the *tuba*. If you're interested, I can show you how my men have learned to make the stuff—we run our trucks on it, and the motors for our battery generators, too."

The colonel's homemade distillery proved to be ingenious enough, but Parsons knew that a more efficient model was available elsewhere. He wrote down, "Small copper still," and promised to send one to MacLish with Spyron's next shipment. Meanwhile, he gave the colonel some firearms, medicine, and radio equipment, and assured him that before long, far larger amounts would be arriving from Australia.

When Parsons returned to the *Narra Maru* for the next leg of his journey, several guerrillas from MacLish's band accompanied him aboard. They had volunteered to man the lonely lookout station that was to be established farther along the coast. The area ahead, though, was reported to be strongly held by the Japanese, and the ship proceeded with even greater caution.

Parsons found his knowledge of local geography extremely valuable now. He remembered that the town of

Surigao was located at the northern tip of Mindanao and that to the right, across a narrow passage of deep water, lay the small island of Dinagat. To the left lay the even smaller island of Panaon, and beyond the latter, the much larger island of Leyte. Between these islands ran the most vital sea lane in the southern and central Philippines—Surigao Strait. No ship could pass through the strait without being seen by an observer concealed on the headlands of Surigao, Dinagat, or Panaon. At one of these sites, the station would have to be established.

But when they put into shore well below the town of Surigao, friendly natives gave them additional information. A strong enemy force was indeed stationed in the area. The Japanese had installed their own observation post on the headlands overlooking the strait, and were using Surigao itself as a naval base. Their patrol launches even then were combing local waters for his ship, which spies had reported sailing along the coast.

Since there was no hope of using Surigao, Parsons' next choice was the island of Panaon. Crossing the narrow stretch of water to reach it, however, promised to be perilous. The *Narra Maru* edged toward Surigao, then hid in the mouth of a neighboring river. After several nights of waiting, the way seemed clear. No enemy ships were patrolling the channel. The launch slipped out, crept through the darkness, and by daybreak had reached the far side of Panaon without being observed by the enemy.

A strange-looking guerrilla force came out to greet them. At first, Parsons thought the natives were wearing yellow warpaint. Questioning one of their leaders, he learned that most of the people on the island were suffering from tropical ulcers. When a large enemy mine had floated ashore recently, a few reckless spirits had decided to see if it might not contain something to alleviate their festering sores. The guerrillas removed the detonators—a terribly dangerous proceeding—and scooped out the explosive powder, which they smeared over their bodies. By chance the powder contained a healing ingredient, and the guerrillas were now in much better health. With a shudder, Parsons added a note to his growing list—"Medicine for tropical ulcers."

High up on the headland of Panaon, he found an ideal site for the coast-watcher station. He left one of Spyron's radio's there, with MacLish's volunteers to operate it. Then he turned north again, toward the island of Leyte.

It was always hazardous to enter previously unexplored territory. The enemy might emerge from any direction without warning. And there was another danger. The *Narra Maru* appeared to be a Japanese ship. Therefore, when she was brought into a presumably friendly harbor or beach, the Rising Sun had to be struck quickly and the Stars and Stripes run up in its place. If the operation took too long, guerrillas hiding on shore were very likely to open fire, and sometimes they were armed with powerful weapons.

Parsons had only a sketchy idea of what he might find on Leyte. Reports said that it was lightly held by the Japanese, but no one knew the exact location of their garrisons. Before proceeding around the strategic island, he decided to seek more information.

He felt particularly uneasy about entering a narrow

stretch of water, scarcely a hundred feet wide, called Panaon Strait. To reach the northern coast of Leyte, the launch would have to pass through the strait, and Parsons couldn't help wondering if the Japanese might not have posted a lookout somewhere above the extremely narrow passage. To be on the safe side, he ordered the launch to anchor below a town on the south coast. Then he went ashore to see what he could learn.

He discovered that he had made a fortunate decision. Meeting a local guerrilla officer, he was told that Panaon Strait certainly was being watched—but not by the enemy. "It's a good thing you stopped here first," the officer told him. "Up north, they always have some of their men guarding the heights. Just last week they caught a Japanese launch like yours in the passage, sank it, and killed everyone aboard."

The officer told Parsons he would be glad to notify the guerrilla force in the north that the *Narra Maru* was approaching and, because she was a friendly vessel, should be allowed safe passage. The southern and northern guerrilla forces on Leyte, the officer explained, kept in touch by means of a "pony express" service. Runners were posted at two-mile intervals, all along the trail linking the two sections. A message would reach someone in the north well before the *Narra Maru*.

Parsons thanked the officer, and returned to the launch. They weighed anchor and moved north again, toward Panaon Strait. Several hours later, as they neared the narrow entrance between the hills, Parsons told the helmsman to turn the wheel. They were ahead of schedule. Why not stop and pay a call at the small village on the nearby shore, before entering the strait?

As they drew near the dock they were greeted by a sharp burst of small-arms fire. The ship was struck several times. Fuel from the punctured drums spilled on deck; luckily, no one was hit. Parsons ordered the ship to keep to its course. Despite the American flag they were flying, a second volley narrowly missed the ship. One of the crew shouted, "Stop! We're friends!" Only then did the firing end.

At the town pier, they were met by a very apologetic American lieutenant. "I'm sorry my men fired at your ship, Commander," he said. "But the only launches we've seen around here have all been Japanese."

"Didn't you get word from the south," Parsons asked him, "telling you we were coming?"

The lieutenant handed him the message he had received from the "pony express." Clearly, in passing from runner to runner, it had lost some of its original meaning.

Parsons read the words: *Look out for a launch arriving this afternoon.*

"And so you thought we were the Nips."

"Yes, sir, we did," the lieutenant said. "And if you hadn't come in here first—well, about an hour ago I put three-quarters of my men up on the heights, ready to blast anything out of the water that tried to sail through."

For a second time, caution had turned the *Narra Maru* away from disaster. It was late spring, and Parsons wrote in his journal: *I have been fired upon by friends many more times than by the enemy.* Fortunately, he was not fired on, at pointblank range, in Panaon Strait.

10

KANGLEON,
PENDATUN AND FERTIG

WHILE ORGANIZING THE PHILIPPINE GUERRILLA MOVE-
ment, Parsons learned that the art of diplomacy often was
of more value than an expert knowledge of military or
naval tactics. Sometimes considerable patience had to be
exercised before a capable leader could be placed in charge
of a particular region. Sometimes tact was required to weed
out troublemakers or to persuade a proud and independent
officer to accept a subordinate role. All too often, if such
measures were not taken, an area would remain in chaos,
and the only one to benefit would be the enemy.

On Leyte, Parsons found no overall authority. There
were several major guerrilla bands, each with its own
leader. The large island was occupied by about three
hundred Japanese soldiers; and with little or nothing to fear

from the enemy, some of the local groups were beginning to turn against one another in their struggle for control.

It was plain that a vigorous, able, and respected officer was needed to unify the area. Parsons made inquiries among his many friends and acquaintances on Leyte. The advice he received was always the same. The only man for the job was Colonel Kangleon.

Before the war, Colonel Ruperto Kangleon had been one of the highest-ranking officers in the Philippine Army, and the District Commander of Samar and Leyte. After the fall of the Islands, he had been imprisoned in a Japanese camp at Butuan, on Mindanao. A force of guerrillas under Colonel MacLish had attacked the camp and freed the prisoners. Colonel Kangleon had crossed to Leyte, and now was living on his farm at San Roque, near the southern tip of the island.

Parsons immediately left for San Roque, where he found the Philippine officer recuperating from his prison ordeal. The colonel listened attentively while Parsons described General MacArthur's hopes for the guerrilla movement in the central and southern islands, but he shook his head when asked if he would be willing to take command of the forces on Leyte.

"My health is not strong," he said. "I wish only to rest here with my wife and children. It shouldn't be difficult to find another officer who can do the job."

"You know the country better than anyone else," Parsons told him. "And the soldiers respect you."

"Thank you, Commander, for your kind words," the colonel said. "But I'm tired of war. And I must confess that

I'm disgusted with the behavior of some of my own countrymen here on Leyte—and with some of yours."

"You've heard about our young American officers?"

"Who hasn't? What sense is there in guerrilla fighting guerrilla? Our real enemy is the Japanese."

"That's exactly why I'm here," Parsons said: "to put an end to this petty squabbling. The island needs a strong leader, Colonel, and all my friends on Leyte, including the Cuenco brothers—both the representative and the Cabinet minister—agree that you are the only one who can fill the role."

"Ah? You have talked with *los* Cuencos?"

Parsons nodded silently, knowing he had scored an important point.

"But I am no longer young," the colonel said. "I believe that such a leader should be a young man."

"Now, there I can't agree with you," Parsons told him. "What's needed is someone who has the respect both of the soldiers and the civilian population. None of the junior officers here on Leyte can make that claim. And I'm sure about one thing: Without the wholehearted support of the people, no guerrilla movement can operate successfully. Once a leader gets on the outs with the ordinary farmers, shopkeepers, and professional men in a district, his days are pretty well numbered. Before long a Japanese patrol is going to learn where he is—and then, no more leader."

"Yes, I know that's true," the colonel said. He frowned thoughtfully. "But the problem here is more complicated, Commander. Supplies and weapons . . . so much is needed. . . ."

"When I get back to Australia," Parsons said, "Spyron will swing into high gear. Small arms will pour into the Islands until every guerrilla will have at least his own tommy gun or carbine."

"Many of the men on Leyte are using old Enfields or Springfields now, or homemade shotguns and captured Japanese rifles."

"Ammunition of every kind also will be brought in."

"The guerrilla soldiers are short of *everything*, Commander. I'm told they're refilling shells with powder from 'duds,' plus Chinese firecracker powder. They're forced to make do with tinfoil, potash permangenate, and matchbox scrapings for fuses."

"Powder," Parsons said, "caps, fuses—they're on my list; and radio stations, generators, uniforms, medicine. . . ."

"You really believe you can bring all those things here in your submarines?"

"I'm sure of it," Parsons said. "General MacArthur and Admiral Kincaid have been behind Spyron from the very beginning. The army will procure the equipment the guerrillas need. The navy will bring it here in cargo-carrying subs."

Unconsciously, the colonel had straightened up in his chair. His eyes were glowing. Parsons knew he had scored further points, and now prepared to play his ace.

"But these supplies, Colonel, will not be given to wildcat guerrilla groups, so that they can fight one another with better weapons, while ignoring the Japanese. They will be delivered only to those areas where we are sure a strong and effective guerrilla movement is in operation."

"And how will you be able to judge if such a movement *is* effective?" the colonel asked him.

"That will be very simple. No guerrilla movement is any better, or any worse, than its leader."

The colonel looked at him for a second or two, and then turned to stare at the neighboring hills. "You really think that I am the only man who can unite the forces here on Leyte?"

"I do."

"Then apparently," Colonel Kangleon said, "this is not the time for an old soldier to rest. You have made my duty clear, Commander Parsons. I have no choice. You may tell General MacArthur I am ready to serve."

And that was the moment when Chick Parsons knew the strategic island of Leyte was in proper hands.

A few weeks later, on his return to southern Mindanao, Parsons decided the time had come to tackle the problem of "Brigadier General" Salipada Pendatun. Although Colonel Fertig had sent a number of new messages, Pendatun still refused to bring his men into Fertig's organization or to recognize the latter's appointment as commander of the island.

"I'd better visit Pendatun's headquarters," Parsons said. "Maybe if I appear in person he'll start to see the light."

"Going there could be pretty dangerous," Fertig said. "He's got three or four thousand well-armed men. I can radio Bowler, though, and have him provide you with an escort."

Parsons shook his head. "That would be asking for

trouble. I'll take a guide, and go in alone." The next morning, dressed in his usual navy cap, sandals, and shorts, Parsons set out to meet the Moro leader.

By following little-known trails, he arrived within a few days at Pendatun's camp in the Del Monte Valley. The short, spare "general" cut a striking figure. "How do I know you are really from MacArthur?" he asked, tapping one of his shiny cavalry boots with a riding crop. "You tell me you are—but where is the proof?"

Parsons took several items out of his knapsack. The Filipino's eyes widened as he was shown a supply of atabrine tablets, American candy, cigarettes, chewing gum, and a fairly recent copy of *Time* magazine.

"These are just a sample," Parsons said. "Join Colonel Fertig, under General MacArthur's authority, and you'll soon be receiving rifles, ammunition, radio sets—everything your men need."

"And what would my rank be?" Pendatun asked.

"Major."

The Filipino leader frowned. "I am a brigadier general! I have a 'pony express,' a radio station and my own army. Why should I join Fertig? My soldiers have plenty of guns, and they know how to use them. We are about to attack the Japanese. We will soon have them surrounded. Come with me, and I will show you how Pendatun deals with the enemy!"

Evidently it was not Pendatun's intention to fight a "regular" guerrilla war. The fiery Filipino officer had sworn to attack the Japanese wherever he found them, and now at least a thousand of his men were on their way to Malaybalay, the capital of the local province, to mount an assault on the enemy garrison.

Parsons began to size up the situation. Almost at once he saw that there was much to be said for the Moro leader's point of view. Pendatun did possess a large and seemingly fine organization. Many Filipino officers from all over Mindanao were serving under him, and so were several excellent American officers. Clearly he commanded a formidable guerrilla army, and naturally enough had no wish to give up his initiative or independence.

Parsons decided to rely on patience and good humor to win Pendatun over. At all costs the guerrilla leader's pride had to be handled with care. He had recently moved into the Del Monte Valley; obviously he was very anxious to impress the natives of the region with his military prowess. The only thing to do was to let him run things in his own way, and from time to time, if there was an opportunity to do so, point out the advantages he would gain by joining Spyron and serving under Fertig and MacArthur.

When Pendatun's soldiers entered Malaybalay, they discovered the Japanese garrison entrenched behind the thick, concrete walls of the local school building. At first, Parsons tried to induce the Filipino leader to withdraw. "Even if you knock out this particular garrison," he said, "far larger forces will soon appear. They'll take revenge not only against your own men but also against the innocent people who live in the town."

Pendatun was unwilling to listen. He had ambitious plans. "My soldiers," he said, "already have blown up the bridges between Malaybalay and the next Japanese garrison in Cagayan. There will be no retaliation. And when we have eliminated the enemy here, we shall attack Cagayan itself. After that, Davao! Eventually I intend to free this entire area from the Japanese!"

Parsons kept still. Some men learned quickly; others —even the best of leaders—needed a little more time.

When the school had been completely surrounded, Pendatun gave the order to fire. Round after round of rifle bullets bounced harmlessly off the concrete walls. The Japanese could be heard laughing, and shouting derisively. Then they opened up with a few machine-gun bursts.

Pendatun's face grew red. "Prepare the bombs and catapults!" he shouted.

The guerrillas, Parsons saw, had built the catapults from inner tubing and bamboo. Their incendiary bombs were made out of beer bottles, filled with gasoline. When the fuses had been lighted, the order to commence firing was given. The bottles flew through the air, to shatter harmlessly against the school walls—those of the incendiaries that even got that far.

"Regular bombs!" Pendatun ordered, his face growing darker. Parsons was surprised to see some of the guerrillas dash off into the jungle, to return shortly afterward lugging fifty- and hundred-pound aerial bombs.

"Where did you get those?" he asked.

"I told you I had everything," Pendatun said. "My men found the bombs at an airfield and hid them away at the time of the surrender. We have dynamite detonators, too, taken from the gold mines. Now you'll see how we knock a hole in that building!"

Pendatun's men removed the regular detonators, inserted those designed to explode dynamite, and then added a safety fuse to each bomb. Parsons was afraid, though, that Pendatun's prestige was likely to suffer another blow. His men were fearless, it was true; crouching low, they carried the bombs and catapults toward the school building; but the Japanese machine-gun fire was too intense for them. They couldn't get close enough to the walls to use the catapults effectively. The bombs arched toward the school, and exploded with a shattering roar. Shrapnel burst against the concrete, but there was no real damage. Truly, the Filipino leader was in a humiliating position. He had the enemy soldiers outnumbered ten to one, but couldn't dislodge them from their little fortress.

"A few American mortars," Parsons said quietly, "a bazooka or two, perhaps a small fieldpiece, such as Spyron hopes to deliver to the recognized guerrilla commanders . . ."

He let the sentence trail off. He was sure that Pendatun had heard him and that the message had been understood.

It took Pendatun's men the rest of the afternoon to breach the wall of the school. They did so only after strapping a brace of hundred-pound bombs to the sides of a water buffalo and then goading the unfortunate beast toward the school building. The explosion killed the carabao and knocked down a large section of concrete. The Japanese soldiers ran from the building to the nearby hills. Half of them were killed, but the rest escaped and carried the news to distant Cagayan, ensuring the eventual dispatch of a large retaliatory force to Malaybalay.

After his hard-won "victory," Pendatun looked rather crestfallen. What sort of figure did he cut now before the local population, a guerrilla leader forced to depend on a lowly water buffalo to defeat the enemy? And how hollow his ambitions sounded—capture Cagayan, Davao, and drive the Japanese from the entire area, when he could hardly manage to drive a detachment out of the local schoolhouse?

For several more days Parsons remained with Pendatun's forces, and waited patiently for the proud Filipino to change his mind. He complimented Pendatun on his excellent staff officers, and the bravery of his men. He also praised Pendatun for the initiative he had shown in organizing his forces in the Del Monte Valley. His soldiers were living off the land, and were no trouble or expense to the local population. They were growing their own vegetables, their own pineapples, and were raising chickens, cattle, and pigs they had brought with them into the region.

A combination of praise and honest criticism, combined with the promise of future "aid," to be gained by joining forces with Colonel Fertig, finally had their effect on the guerrilla leader. One evening, Pendatun took off his gold star and replaced it with the gold oak leaf Parsons gave him. He saluted, and said, "I will serve under MacArthur."

Parsons returned his salute. "Major, I know that back in Australia, the general will be very pleased." It was the truth. For Pendatun was one of the best of all the Filipino leaders, and his force of several thousand men added a strong new element to the guerrilla movement already organized and in the field on Mindanao.

11

A RUDE
AWAKENING

BY NOW, THROUGHOUT THE CENTRAL AND SOUTHERN islands, guerrilla soldiers were attacking the Japanese. Many underground leaders already had learned the lesson of Malaybalay: that it is wasteful and foolish to mount an assault against an entrenched enemy. The Filipino irregular was at home in the jungle. Even with limited firepower he could successfully harass or ambush a stronger force, inflict a number of casualties, and then fade back into the forests, where the enemy was reluctant to follow. The result of such efforts was becoming quite clear. Japanese planes scattered thousands of new surrender leaflets over any rural area in which guerrilla forces were thought to be concentrating.

A few days after his return to Colonel Fertig's command, Parsons went along as an observer on a typical jungle ambush. While the guerrilla squad glided through the forest, their young American lieutenant, a West Point graduate, explained the background of the operation.

The Japanese in the area, he said, were using huge trucks, almost as big as boxcars, to supply and relieve their various outposts. In peacetime, the trucks had belonged to a company that grew and processed sugarcane. Then the enemy had come, confiscated the trucks, and converted them into military personnel carriers, by adding boiler plate around the sides and back.

Guerrilla observers posted along the jungle road had made an interesting discovery. The Japanese always sent their trucks out at the same time of day. They never varied the schedule. Now, a relief force of fifty enemy soldiers would soon appear, and his own squad would be ready for them.

The site selected for the ambush was in a thickly wooded mountain section. The forest would permit his squad to approach unseen, and to retreat to safety if the operation misfired. When they arrived at the road, Parsons saw three young guerrillas, with tommy guns and automatic rifles, slip away from the rest of the squad. They took up positions on one side of the road, behind trees and bushes.

"They'll fire," the lieutenant said, "into the windshield, tires, and motor, bringing the truck to a halt within fifty feet."

"But how can you be sure the truck will stop inside a specified distance?" Parsons asked him.

The lieutenant shrugged. "Because that's what the trucks always do."

Parsons watched the rest of the guerrillas as they began

to dig a long trench on the side of the road opposite the three hidden tommy gunners. They dug it fifty feet from the trio, where the lieutenant had said the truck would stop. When the trench was deep enough, the squad concealed it with a covering of sod and grass, and then took up hidden positions in the thick undergrowth.

The lieutenant then told Parsons there was nothing for them to do but wait. He led the way to a small hill nearby, out of the line of fire. From there, they would have a complete view of the action below.

Parsons thought of something else. "All your men, except for the three tommy gunners," he said, "are on the same side of the road. What's the point of that?"

"I put them there," the lieutenant explained, "because the Japanese come out on the side away from the original volley. Always."

A short distance off, through the forest, the sound of a heavy truck could be heard, laboring up the jungle road.

"Tell me," Parsons asked, "if the truck is armor-plated, why don't the Nips just stay inside, and fight off your men from there?"

"Apparently claustrophobia hits them," the lieutenant said. "Their only thought is to get out of the truck and behind something immobile, like a tree, from where they can return our fire. Or maybe it's just panic that gets them."

"But if they stayed inside," Parsons said, "they could use a shortwave radio to call for reinforcements, holding your men off till help arrived."

"They *could,*" the lieutenant said. "But fortunately they

don't. The Japanese are very obliging. You'll see, in another minute or two."

The huge truck came into sight, crawling up the grade. Large geysers of steam spurted from under the radiator cap. The three guerrillas with automatic rifles waited until they could see the peaked caps of the driver and his mechanic. Then they opened fire.

The windshield of the truck cracked and splintered. The engine coughed, snorted, and coughed again. The tires burst. There were frightened screams inside, as the truck weaved back and forth along the road. Finally it halted, exactly where the lieutenant had said it would.

A swarm of green uniforms poured from the back of the truck. Desperately seeking concealment, the enemy soldiers raced to the side of the road, and tumbled into the hidden trench. At the same moment, guerrillas in tattered shirts rose up from their jungle cover, and raced down the hill. Rifles rang out, and long, razor-sharp bolos glinted in the sun.

In a minute, it was all over. Within five, not a piece of equipment or a stitch of clothing remained on the victims in the trench. A few more rifles had been added to the local guerrillas' arsenal, a few more casualties added to the toll exacted by the jungle fighters.

Parsons compared the day's activities with what he had seen at Malaybalay. Afterward he added a note to his journal: "I am definitely a guerrilla. I see no sense in risking annihilation in open combat when you can fight, kill, run —and, later, fight again."

By late June, 1943, Parsons knew that his secret mission

to the Philippines would soon draw to an end. He had been living behind enemy lines four months, with the danger of imprisonment and death never very far away. The risks had been justified, though. A network of Spyron coast-watcher stations was established, and the guerrilla movement had been consolidated and strengthened. After completing a last, short swing through parts of central Mindanao, it would be time for him to return to Colonel Fertig's headquarters, send out a request for a submarine, and then report back to General MacArthur in Australia.

Everywhere on his travels, Parsons had been treated with characteristic Filipino hospitality. Arriving now in the town of Jimenez, he was given another cordial reception. The family of an old friend, Senator Ozamis, took him into their adobe house high above the beach. For several days he was able to enjoy the luxury of good food, electric lights, hot water, and a comfortable room where he could put in order some of the notes he had been making during his mission.

There were no enemy soldiers stationed in Jimenez, but less than twenty miles away the Japanese had built a navy patrol base. Nearly every evening some of their ships went out. As soon as one of them appeared in neighboring waters, the guerrilla sentries posted on the beach at Jimenez sounded the alarm. Iron would clang on iron, while the townspeople hastily gathered up some of their possessions and fled to the hills. There they would remain until the all clear sounded. Occasionally a patrol boat did land a squad of soldiers at Jimenez, but most times the warning turned out to be a false alarm.

One evening Parsons was seated at his desk, working on

the report he was preparing, when he heard the alarm sounding in the village. The Ozamis family began to scurry about, collecting a few essentials to carry off with them. The youngest daughter tapped on his door. *"Vamos, chico,"* she said. "We must leave again."

Parsons stretched his arms, and yawned. "Every night we leave for nothing," he complained. "Those boys down on the beach are just too jumpy."

"It is better to be too jumpy," the girl said, "than to hang by your thumbs."

Involuntarily, Parsons looked down at his right hand. "That's true," he said. "You go ahead with the others, and before long I'll catch up with you." He heard her going down the stairs. The front door closed. Then it grew silent again in the adobe house.

He sat at the desk and reviewed the summary he had been making. Mindanao—in excellent shape, thanks to Fertig, Hedges, Pendatun, and the other leaders. Leyte, now under Kangleon—improving rapidly, with news coming in almost every day, indicating good progress there.

Panay—he hadn't been able to pay a personal call on Major Macario Peralta, whose original message had signaled the outbreak of guerrilla warfare, but radio reports tended to suggest a strong, united force at work on the island, causing the Japanese a great deal of trouble. Major Peralta would most likely receive Spyron supplies before very much longer.

Samar, Negros, Bohol, Cebu—confused rivalries, officers quarreling among themselves, problems that could only be resolved at a later time.

"Nevertheless," he wrote, "there are vigorous, potentially useful guerrilla groups on all the important southern and central islands. The law of the survival of the fittest will solve some of these situations. Others I will endeavor to handle on my next trip."

Luzon—probably the Japanese forces were too strong to permit an open guerrilla effort, but according to Senator Ozamis, it might soon be possible to organize a spy network in Manila. . . .

The general picture in the Islands was excellent. A free movement existed. It was widespread, and growing larger every month. It had the support of great sections of the civilian population, and its ranks were filling with thousands of young Filipino soldiers, eager to engage in a struggle for national liberation. With supplies from Spyron, the Underground would become an ever-increasing threat to the occupation forces, compelling the Japanese to divert soldiers and arms, which they badly needed elsewhere, to the main islands of the archipelago. And when the American invasion landings began, the guerrillas would be a vital factor in the struggle against a well entrenched enemy. . . .

Parsons put down his pencil, turned off the shaded lamp, and parted the blackout curtain. Silence lay over the deserted town. At the base of the cliff, in a flood of tropical moonlight, the waves of the sea broke slowly and peacefully against the shore. There was no sign of the enemy. The sentries had been too apprehensive again. Another false alarm.

No bed had ever looked so comfortable as the one in the

corner of the darkened room. After weeks of tramping along jungle trails, of countless nights stretched out on thin mats or on the bare ground, the temptation to remain was irresistible. He kicked off his sandals, undressed, and two minutes later was dead to the world.

At dawn he was awakened by someone pounding on the front door. The Ozamis family must have forgotten their keys when they'd gone up to the hills. Now they were back, asking to be let in. He put on his clothes again and started down the stairs. Halfway there, he stopped to look out of the window.

It wasn't the Ozamis family.

A Japanese truck was parked by the curb. A half-dozen armed soldiers were pounding on the door.

Parsons dashed back to the bedroom and began to cram his papers into a knapsack. Everything was there—maps, reports, official documents, even letters from various guerrilla leaders to General MacArthur. If the dossier fell into enemy hands, it would mean not only his own death but also the death of thousands of Filipino and American soldiers who had trusted him. It would cripple Spyron before it had begun to operate freely, and might even destroy the entire guerrilla movement in the Islands.

There was no time to blame himself for carelessness and stupidity. The sounds at the front door were growing louder. The Japanese were shouting violently, and hammering with their fists. Soon they would smash their way in.

Parsons tried to remember the layout of the adobe house. On the ground floor were a large warehouse area, and a smaller room where different commodities also were stored. Neither contained a hiding place. Here, on the second floor, were the family's living and sleeping quarters. Glancing above his head, he saw an opening that led to the attic. It was too high to reach, though, without placing a couple of chairs on top of the dining-room table. And suppose he did climb into the attic that way—how was he to draw the chairs up after him, so the Japanese wouldn't realize someone was hiding there?

The attic was useless. No other place in the house offered any hope of concealment. He had to leave. The only way out was by the kitchen. If the soldiers hadn't arrived there yet, he might still have a chance.

For a moment the hammering stopped. Then another sound replaced it. One of the soldiers must have found an ax. The splintering of wood grew louder.

Clutching his knapsack, Parsons dashed down the rear staircase. The soldiers were attacking the front door with great fury. He peered over the windowsill. The backyard looked empty. Edging the door open, he stepped outside.

Silence. Nothing moved. He took a deep breath, then raced through the yard, placed a hand on the fence, and vaulted over.

The alley was deserted. The soldiers hadn't thought of coming around to the back. He began to run toward the coconut groves, and didn't stop running until he had reached the safety of the hills.

12

THE
START SOUTH

THE SOLDIERS WHO NEARLY HAD CAPTURED PARSONS IN
the town of Jimenez had not been conducting a routine
patrol. They were part of a new force of several thousand
men, assembled and sent into the field to destroy Colonel
Fertig's guerrilla movement. The Japanese had grown
weary of persuasion. Millions of leaflets and hundreds of
radio broadcasts had failed to induce Fertig's Filipino soldiers to surrender their arms. Now the Japanese swarmed
ashore at a dozen landing places on Mindanao, compelling
the colonel to withdraw north and east, into the mountains.

As a result, Parsons found himself cut off in enemy-held
territory. Using a native guide, he set out cautiously along
backcountry trails. After several days he managed to slip

through the Japanese lines. Reaching Colonel Fertig's jungle camp, he received a particularly warm welcome.

"I knew you'd been trapped by the landings," the colonel told him, as they sat together on the steps of guerrilla headquarters. "When you didn't show up after three or four days, it looked like you'd been captured for sure. We notified Australia. They've listed you as missing in action."

Parsons described his narrow escape in Jimenez, and his journey through the backcountry to safety. Then he said that he wanted a message sent to General MacArthur, requesting a submarine. "With your men up here in the north," he told the colonel, "the area along the southern coast should be relatively free of Japanese. That's where Charley Smith and I will rendezvous with our sub."

"I'll get the message out," Fertig said. "And I've got three passengers for you to take along to Australia. They're American officers who've just escaped from Davao prison camp. General MacArthur wants them pretty badly. They've got a lot of tales to tell about prisoner of war treatment."

"Are they in condition to walk?" Parsons asked him. "We'll have plenty of ground to cover, and some of the terrain might get a bit rugged."

"I think they'll be able to make it," Fertig said. "I've been feeding them up since they reached camp. Oh— somebody else walked in here the other day. I imagine you'll be glad to see him."

The colonel turned with a smile, and shouted, "You can come out now, Captain," and a thin young man in a faded uniform stepped onto the porch. Parsons could hardly believe his eyes. It was his brother-in-law, Tommy Jurika.

Several moments passed before they said anything. It was such an improbable meeting. To arrive at this jungle clearing on Mindanao, one of them had fled from a prisoner of war camp several hundred miles away, while the other had spent a year escaping from Manila and circling the globe.

Then they began to talk about all that had happened to them since the fall of the Islands. "The whole family seems to have been on the move lately," Tommy finally said. Suddenly his eyes turned sober. "I'm glad Katsy and the boys are fine—but I heard that my mother didn't go with you."

"She stuck around. . . ."

"Because of me. Sure, I knew what she'd do, when she heard I was taken prisoner. Well, I guess that's where I head next. Manila."

Parsons studied his brother-in-law. Tommy was only twenty-eight, but he knew the Islands almost as well as any man alive. "I have something else for you to do," he said. "A bigger job, because it will affect more people. If I say I'll make every effort to get your mother out of Manila, will you join my staff?"

"Where would I be working?"

"At advance Spyron bases, once they're set up. Next time I leave here, I'd like to bring you out with me."

"Fine—as long as you take care of that other matter. You know the way news travels, Chick. In another few months, Manila might not be too healthy for the mother-in-law of Commander Parsons."

"I'm already working on it."

"Okay," Tommy Jurika said. "Then Spyron's got itself another man. I'll stay here with the colonel till you want me."

By the end of the week, Parsons had completed his plans for reaching the coast. Headquarters in Australia had agreed to divert a submarine, the rendezvous to take place on the sixth day. If all went well, the trek south would require no more than five; he added an extra twenty-four hours to the schedule, just to be safe.

Their party consisted of several young Filipino guerrillas from Colonel Fertig's command, who were to act as guides and porters, and five Americans: Parsons, Charley Smith, and the three ex-prisoners. The youngest of the three was Colonel William Dyess, an aviator who had survived the Bataan Death March. The other two were Lieutenant Commander Melvin McCoy and Colonel Stephen Melnick, both taken prisoner at the fall of Corregidor.

Among them, the members of the party had only one tommy gun, two pistols, and a small amount of ammunition. They carried little food, for they hoped to find a number of friendly *barrios,* or native villages, along the way. They possessed almost no medicine, and just one canteen for water. The most important item in their baggage was Parsons' complete dossier on the guerrilla movement. By now, it was literally worth its weight in gold.

If he felt any special concern as they set out on their journey, it was over the stamina of the three ex-prisoners. Parsons knew that Dyess, McCoy, and Melnick all had been in Japanese camps for more than a year, living under appalling conditions. Now, in uncertain health after their ordeal, they might easily find the unmapped terrain too much for their strength.

On the first day Parsons planned to reach camp by 3:00 or 4:00 P.M. Until noon they made excellent progress along the well-marked jungle trail. Then, arriving at a deep, crocodile-infested stream, they found the only bridge destroyed. Parts of it, in fact, were still burning, but since no Japanese soldiers were believed to be in the area, they assumed the destruction had been the work of local guerrillas.

Fortunately, some of the timbers remained undamaged. While two men stood guard to keep off any inquisitive crocodiles, the rest of the party plunged into the water and lashed the timbers together with jungle creepers. Using this makeshift raft, they managed to ferry themselves safely across to the opposite side of the stream.

They were now several hours late, and when five o'clock came, they still had not arrived at the first barrio. They felt desperately tired. Heads down, they trudged along the jungle path, scarcely looking where they were going. Suddenly, around a bend, they almost stumbled into a native village. After pausing for a second or two, Colonel Dyess let out a yell. A number of enemy soldiers were there, taking a bath in somebody's backyard.

At the same moment the Japanese saw them, and began to scuttle around the yard in a wild hunt for their guns and uniforms. By the time the enemy soldiers had located their weapons, Parsons and the rest of the party had fled, plunging back into the jungle along a secondary trail that led up the side of a mountain.

After that, everything seemed to go wrong. As they raced ahead to throw off pursuit, it began to rain. The trail grew wet and muddy, and while they slipped and fell and picked themselves up again, night finally settled over the jungle.

It took four or five more hours to reach a small clearing near the top of the mountain. In the darkness, they could see rows of ripe corn. They hadn't eaten all day; as they passed, they pulled off some of the ears, and ate them raw. The corn, everyone agreed, tasted delicious.

Beyond the field they came to a small bamboo hut. It was filled with people from the barrio at the foot of the mountain—the one where the Japanese soldiers had been doing their bathing. The villagers said that an enemy patrol of about fifty men had come to the barrio early in the morning and that they themselves had just managed to escape. Although they did not have much food, they willingly shared their small supply with Parsons and the others. Three chickens didn't go very far when it had to be divided among more than a dozen hungry soldiers, but even a morsel of cooked food was better than nothing.

Before he fell asleep that night, Parsons took stock of their position. As yet they were not too far off schedule, but the presence of Japanese soldiers in the area was extremely disturbing. It meant that from now on they would have to exercise much greater caution, and probably would make even slower progress as a result. Naturally, though the paramount consideration was to keep away from enemy patrols, they couldn't afford to fall too far behind. The submarine would not wait if they failed to keep the rendezvous. Taking one thing with another, it was hardly a pleasant picture to fall asleep on.

13

JUNGLE
FLIGHT

IN THE MORNING, THE VILLAGERS PRODUCED MORE BAR-
becued chicken for breakfast, and one of their number, who
claimed to be an excellent guide, offered to lead them on
the next part of their journey. He said he could show them a
shortcut over the mountain that would take them back to
the main trail. From there they quickly could reach the
more distant barrio, in which they originally had planned to
spend the second night.

Parsons and the others agreed to accept his offer, and
when breakfast was over they started down the mountain-
side. Most of the morning they crept along, looking for the
trail. After three or four hours spent this way, it became
obvious the guide was completely lost.

Charley Smith, who had the only compass, took the lead.

Their course became even more erratic. They wandered along riverbanks and over the spongy beds of mountain springs, crossing any open space that seemed to lead in the right direction and that did not require cutting a path through the almost impenetrable undergrowth. At last, far behind schedule, they stumbled onto the main trail.

Despite the time lost, their spirits rose. By slipping across the mountain, they felt sure they had eluded the Japanese patrol and were now safe from pursuit. A few members of the party even sang or whistled as they swung along, until Charley Smith, who was in the lead, stopped short. He pointed down at the trail. There in the soft mud were several imprints of a rubber sole, with the so-called "tabby," or one-toe, design. It was the sole used only by the Japanese Army.

Apparently the enemy patrol had been more clever than they had supposed. It had split up into two squads, one swinging around the base of the mountain, the other going over the top. In fact, the second squad must have gone past them that morning, while they themselves had been taking their "shortcut." The positions were now reversed. The enemy was in the lead, and Parsons and his companions were following along behind.

Because there was only a single trail through this part of the jungle, they had no choice but to keep to it, hoping by the exercise of extreme caution to avoid an ambush. Two of the guerrillas promptly removed their uniforms so that they would look like local natives. Then the young soldiers went on ahead, as scouts, ready to alert the rest of the party if they saw the Japanese patrol.

The guerrillas were remarkably casual about the dangerous situation. At about three o'clock in the afternoon they were so close on the heels of the enemy that someone found a Japanese cigarette butt, still glowing, by the side of the muddy trail. One guerrilla picked it up, took a few puffs, and threw it aside with disdain. "It's Jap, not American," he said. "I do not like it!"

They moved forward again, and after several minutes began to approach an open space at the top of a hill. Suddenly an old Moro woman rose out of the tall grass. No one in the party could speak her dialect, but her gestures soon made the message clear. She had been asked by some Japanese if she had seen any Americans along the trail. Putting two and two together, she had reasoned that there were Americans around *somewhere*. She had hidden in the grass, to warn them if they came by. She had done so only because of her hatred of the enemy—and at no small risk to herself.

They thanked the old woman, and then edged forward to the top of the hill. Below, resting comfortably in a grove of palm trees, were the Japanese soldiers. They were lying about, eating their rations, and washing everything down with coconut milk.

Parsons and the others had had no food since early morning. The sight of the Japanese, eating and drinking, was almost too much to bear. They retired to the tall grass and held a conference. Charley Smith was all for attacking the soldiers. A count of their bullets, however, proved the plan unfeasible. Even if each bullet killed an enemy, half the patrol would still be left. There was no choice but to remain hidden, and to wait and see what the patrol would do next.

Cautiously they stretched out on the top of the hill and crammed their mouths full of leaves to quiet their hunger pangs. They could see that the trail divided, below the grove. If the Japanese took the fork to the left, things would begin to look brighter. But if the patrol went straight ahead, they themselves would have to follow, and continue to run the risk of being ambushed.

Finally the Japanese moved on—and took the fork to the left. As soon as they were out of sight, Parsons and the rest raced down the other path. For several hours they moved quickly forward. They knew that almost an entire day had been wasted and that they were falling more and more behind time. The worst of it was, they did not have a radio to communicate with the guerrilla forces ahead or to make direct contact with the submarine. The rendezvous was set, and they had no way of requesting a postponement.

At dusk they found a native house, only recently deserted. Colonel Dyess ran down a stray chicken, which they killed and cooked. A collection of green papayas, some corn, and a few *camotes,* or sweet potatoes, made up the rest of their frugal meal. They felt an additional need to make haste, and they plunged along the trail again, until they were too exhausted to continue. It was all too probable that the enemy patrol, having found no trace of them along the left fork, had doubled back by now and picked up their trail again. If such were the case, it was doubtful that they had put enough distance between themselves and their pursuers.

The night was pitch black by the time they dragged their feet off the jungle path, lay down on some blankets, and fell into a fitful sleep.

Conditions grew even worse on the third day. The wet jungle trails were as difficult as any that Parsons had seen during his travels in the Islands. Mostly they consisted of thick, slimy mud through which the party kept floundering, one man after another sinking in up to his knees. Parsons, his feet quite tough, walked barefoot, and suffered far less than his fellow Americans. The other four wore G.I. shoes, and they had to spend several minutes out of every hour by the side of the trail, removing the gravel that had worked its way inside.

Showers fell during much of the day, and the weather remained extremely hot and humid. Everyone in the party was soaked with rain and sweat. Time and again they came to streams too deep to wade. Then they had to pause, while a raft was built to ferry across their arms, blankets, and Parsons' bundle of vital papers.

At each new clearing in the jungle the heat became fiercer. After a while they developed an almost unendurable thirst. Commander McCoy had brought along a supply of halazone tablets for purifying water, but there was only one small canteen in which to put them, and the process simply took too long for impatient men. Reaching the bank of a dark stream, they flung themselves down and gulped the water, indifferent to the dangers of dysentery or typhoid fever.

As night was falling they came to a rickety barn that held two cows and four small goats. By then the men were ravenous. At first they decided to slaughter one of the cows. No one knew how to go about it, though, and because the animal was so large, they agreed that it might be easier to slaughter one of the goats.

The trouble was that the goats bleated so pitifully, making such a "human" sound, that no one in the party could bring himself to do it. They were still standing in the barn, arguing over the dilemma, when one of the young guerrillas returned from a foraging expedition. He reported finding some natives a half mile away who had offered to cook a pig for their supper.

A detail of men went off, returning shortly afterward with armloads of barbecued pork wrapped in banana leaves, and carrying more banana leaves filled with hot, ground corn, steamed like rice. Parsons and the others ate their fill for the first time in three days. Then they lay down in the barn to snatch a few hours' sleep. The goats bleated all night long, and the cows lowed, but no one minded. Even the guerrillas who stood guard seemed glad that no one had slaughtered any of the barnyard animals.

On the fourth day they awoke at dawn and reheated the leftovers from the previous night's feast. As they were eating breakfast in the barn, they were joined by five guerrillas from the nearby town of Aurora. The guerrillas had fled from an enemy patrol, the same one with which Parsons and his companions had been playing hide-and-seek in the jungle for the past forty-eight hours. According to the guerrillas, the Japanese were now on the trail behind them, and not too far away.

Unhappy to learn about the patrol, but cheered by the addition of five more soldiers to their own ranks—each of the new guerrillas had a rifle and a good supply of ammunition—Parsons and the rest set off at a brisk pace. They made excellent progress for five or six hours, and were growing more confident of meeting their schedule, when they came to a deep, swift-moving river. It was the most difficult they had yet encountered. While the guerrillas fell to work building another bamboo raft, Parsons and Colonel Dyess decided to take a guide and go on ahead. A native in the vicinity had told them of a guerrilla encampment farther along the trail. They hoped to find a radio transmitter there so that they could send a message to the submarine, requesting a delay in the rendezvous.

To cross the swift river, Parsons and the colonel removed their trousers, inflated them with air, and using them as water wings, paddled their way over to the other side. Then they followed the trail through the steaming jungle, not turning or backtracking even once. Two hours later, to their utter discouragement, they found themselves standing on the riverbank, exactly where they had started, watching their companions pole across on the newly finished raft. The guide was not to blame for having taken them in a circle. The expedition had reached a deserted section of the jungle. There were few barrios in which to obtain information, and the trails were so little used that no one knew very much about them.

When the river had been safely crossed, they resumed the march, using Charley Smith's compass again, rather than relying solely on the judgment of the guides. As time went by, the party began to string itself out along the trail. Commander McCoy and one of the young guerrillas were in the lead. They drew farther and farther ahead of the others, until finally, at dusk, Parsons noticed they were no longer in sight.

Night came, but there was still no sign of the guerrilla encampment. Instead, not long after dark, they saw a small village just off the trail. It was deserted except for a very old man and his wife. Parsons and the others ate a light meal, which the couple generously provided from their meager stores. Later, still hungry but almost too weary to care, they rolled up in their blankets and prepared for sleep.

McCoy and his guide had not come back. They were somewhere up ahead in the jungle, and there was no telling what might have happened to them.

Early the next day—the fifth since they had left Colonel Fertig's headquarters—they began to follow the trail again. At noon they finally reached the guerrilla encampment. Commander McCoy and his guide were there, but the ex-prisoner was unable to explain coherently why he had strayed so far ahead of the main party. Parsons could see that he needed rest, and perhaps medical treatment as well. His condition made an immediate rendezvous with the submarine appear even more urgent.

They stayed with the guerrilla forces that afternoon and evening, eating as much as they could in order to regain some of their strength. The last leg of their journey lay before them, and it promised to be taxing. While they slept and relaxed, Captain Medina, the commander of the guerrillas, sent a detachment of his men back up the trail to ambush the enemy patrol. His soldiers returned in time for supper. The Japanese had been put to flight with the loss of ten or twelve men, and there was nothing more to fear, at least from that direction.

Parsons still found several reasons for concern. According to all he had heard the last day or two, there were far stronger enemy forces in the territory just ahead than he had anticipated. Reaching the submarine under the best of circumstances had never promised to be easy. Now the presence of large Japanese contingents in the area, along with McCoy's failing health, did nothing to improve their prospects. To darken the picture even further, there was no transmitter in the guerrilla camp, so Parsons was unable to send word to the submarine, explaining the need for a brief delay. It was with a satisfied stomach, but an uneasy mind, that he said good night to his host and went off to sleep.

The sixth day of the journey began with an early breakfast, and then the party set out once more, after thanking Captain Medina and his men for their invaluable assistance. When they had been on the march several hours, a familiar difficulty arose. The guide completely lost his sense of direction, and they began to wander around the hills and valleys, with no notion whatever of where they really might be.

Charley Smith again took the lead with his compass, but this time it failed to help. They simply could not regain their bearings. There were no landmarks anywhere. The jungle remained featureless, and they did not find a single house or village, even a deserted one, along the trail. The hours passed, and still they met no one on the march. They seemed to have reached a part of the jungle that was, except for themselves, devoid of human life. Wearily they climbed each new hill with the same expectation: From the top they would finally be able to catch a glimpse of the blue waters of the bay. But each time they reached the crest, it was always the same: more green jungle, stretching endlessly ahead.

They kept plodding on doggedly, all morning and most of the afternoon. About four o'clock, one of the guerrillas darted back with the news that he had seen the water. They quickened their pace as much as they could, and soon came to a small village by the shore. Stopping just long enough to gulp down some coconut milk, they staggered ahead, almost totally exhausted, the last two miles to their destination.

A launch was there to greet them. The local guerrilla leader, Captain McCarthy, welcomed them aboard. He said he had been awaiting their arrival for two days. Colonel Fertig had sent him word that Parsons and his party were coming and that it was very possible they might be delayed en route. The captain had attempted to transmit this information to the submarine, but there was no way of knowing if his message had been received. Any submarine lying offshore was extremely vulnerable, and would never reveal its presence by breaking radio silence.

Then the launch carried them to a nearby cove where

Captain McCarthy had built his guerrilla camp. From there, the captain sent another message to the submarine, announcing the arrival of Parsons and his companions, and asking that the time of the rendezvous be changed until late the next afternoon. Because the area was alive with Japanese land and naval patrols—there were far more soldiers and ships around than there had been even a week or two earlier—Captain McCarthy also asked that the rendezvous be held in a different and safer location.

Because the submarine, of course, still did not reply, it was impossible to tell whether the captain's second message had been received, either.

On the seventh morning Parsons awoke early, and checked his maps and papers for what he hoped would be the last time. If everything went well, by nightfall the long trek would be over, and the information he had been gathering during a period of almost half a year would be safely aboard an American submarine.

The final hours, though, would be the most dangerous. To arrive at their rendezvous, he and his four companions would have to leave all cover behind and cross a stretch of open sea, in plain view of the enemy.

And of course, even then, there was the strong possibility that the submarine might not appear. It could very well have left the vicinity the previous night, when he and the others had failed to arrive on schedule. If that were the case, a new rendezvous would have to be arranged, perhaps hundreds of miles away, where enemy forces were not concentrated so heavily. To reach such a site, Parsons knew they would have to take to the backcountry again, and he was almost certain that McCoy, and perhaps one or two of the others, could not survive a second jungle ordeal.

When it grew light, he and Charley Smith and the three ex-prisoners ate breakfast for the last time with their young guerrilla escorts. Afterward, they gave their extra clothing, their arms and ammunition, to the jungle fighters, and then shook hands with them, and said goodbye.

Parsons led the other four down to the water, where they went aboard the launch again. Captain McCarthy's men had camouflaged the ship with vines and coconut fronds, and other leaves, until it looked like a part of the landscape. Keeping very close to shore, they ran the launch slowly from the cove to a nearby island, where they settled down and remained hidden for the rest of the morning and the early part of the afternoon.

At four o'clock it was time to move out. They discarded the leaves and vines, and started the motors. The launch headed away from land. Hopefully, if enemy eyes were watching, they would see nothing suspicious in the small ship's leisurely course.

The site of the rendezvous was five miles offshore, in the middle of the bay. Signals had been agreed on beforehand, to indicate that all was clear. The run out to the rendezvous site was made without incident. The bay seemed completely free of enemy patrols. Parsons and Charley Smith arranged the signals, and then all sat down in the launch to wait.

The minutes ticked away: ten, fifteen, twenty; a half hour. And still no sign.

At first they'd felt reasonably confident that everything

would turn out all right. A submarine had to be cautious in such circumstances. Even when the captain saw their signals, he might want to remain submerged a while longer, just to be absolutely sure it was safe to come up. But as time continued to pass, their optimism faltered. They *had* been a day late—the sub might very well have left, thinking they had not managed to reach the coast. There really was nothing to indicate that it was there, somewhere below the surface of the deserted bay.

An hour, then an hour and a half, went by. The launch rocked gently in the waves. An evening breeze sprang up. The sun fell lower, toward the rim of the horizon.

An hour and three-quarters, and still no sound, no signal. Then two hours, and the sea remained empty.

Just before sunset, the usually calm and unsmiling Charley Smith let out a yell. "There it is!" he shouted, and, astonishingly, threw his arms around Parsons' neck.

Melnick, McCoy, Dyess—all of them—looked across the water, and saw the submarine's conning tower, a few hundred feet away, rising majestically from the sea.

In their weariness, one man burst into tears; another simply stared; a third embraced both Parsons and Smith, and shouted: "She's here! My God, she's here!"

The transfer took only a few minutes. Parsons was the last of the party to leave the launch. As he handed up the dossier of maps and papers, and then climbed aboard himself, he paused for a moment to look back at the distant shore. His secret mission was over—and, incredibly enough, the gamble had been won.

14

$50,000—
DEAD OR ALIVE

DURING THE FOLLOWING MONTHS AN EVER-INCREASING supply of "aid" flowed north, from Australia and New Guinea, to the guerrilla forces in the Philippines. At first, regular fleet submarines were used to transport it. Their capacity was so limited, though, that before long Parsons requested a large cargo-carrying submarine; and eventually two of them were assigned exclusively to Spyron.

Ammunition, firearms, medicine, clothing, and radio equipment made up the ordinary cargoes. But sometimes more unusual items were included in a shipment. Parsons knew the guerrilla leaders—and how a small gesture can mean a great deal to even the flintiest commander. Major Pendatun was inordinately proud of his shiny cavalry boots.

He received a consignment of saddle soap, to keep the boots soft and in good condition.

Colonel Kangleon posed a different problem. He had lost forty pounds while a prisoner of the Japanese, and his gums had shrunk so much that now his false teeth no longer fitted very snugly.

"Teeth stickum," Parsons said, and the item was procured for the commanding officer on Leyte.

Colonel Fertig wanted something else, and wanted it badly. He and his men had long since run out of soap. They had learned how to make a substitute by blending coconut oil with a mixture of burnt coral and wood. The substitute produced a splendid lather, but unfortunately it also turned some men's hair red. Colonel Fertig did not enjoy having red hair. He was sent six bars of toilet soap.

The civilian population and the ordinary guerrilla soldiers in the field also received Spyron's special attention. Enemy propaganda kept repeating that the Americans had deserted their Filipino allies and had no intention of coming back to liberate the Islands. To counter the effects of this claim, and to encourage further resistance, a great number of small, symbolic gifts were brought to the Philippines in Spyron submarines. Cigarettes, chocolate bars, and chewing gum, pencils and sewing kits, arrived on the beaches week after week and quickly passed into thousands of native hands. Stamped on each package and kit were the well-remembered words of General MacArthur: *I shall return.*

Spyron also helped maintain civilian morale through the use of radio broadcasts. Shortwave receivers were distributed widely in guerrilla-held territory, and a few sets were smuggled even into occupied areas, despite the fact that the Kempeitai executed anyone caught listening to clandestine broadcasts.

Parsons learned that between 5:00 and 6:00 P.M., a majority of Islanders could most conveniently reach their local shortwave sets, and at this hour a special program began to be beamed to the Philippines from Australia. Everywhere, people listened eagerly—in rural villages, in the mountains, in coast-watcher huts on lonely hills overlooking the sea, in tiny attics of a thousand city houses, where an informer or an agent of the secret police might be lurking only a few steps away.

First the listeners heard music—the notes of the Philippine national anthem. Then the news broadcast began. The war in Europe, people were told, was drawing to an end. Italy already had surrendered; the Allies had landed in France; and as they advanced against Nazi Germany in the west, Russia's armies were converging on Germany from the east.

In the conflict against Japan, the tide had turned. America and her allies were gaining fresh victories in the central Pacific and in the Dutch East Indies. Enemy garrisons had been cut off, and enemy convoys harassed and sunk. Forward bases were being built closer and closer to the Islands, and new airfields already had placed Mindanao, Leyte, and Samar within bombing range. The day when American soldiers and marines would land on Philippine soil was drawing nearer. And then the voice of General MacArthur, promising to return, brought the program to an end.

For fifteen months, Chick Parsons participated in Spyron's multiple activities. Much of the time he shuttled between the Philippines and bases in Australia, Timor and Borneo. He contracted malaria, and suffered recurrent attacks. He rode the cargo submarines on their dangerous assignments.

During one voyage, after a large enemy tanker had been torpedoed, a pair of escorting destroyers suddenly appeared on the radar screen. The captain took the submarine down, but the Japanese ships moved closer. Depth charges shook the sub, and crockery began to crash in the galley. As the jarring grew stronger, the lights flickered, and bits of paint flaked off and cascaded around their feet.

The captain told Parsons that their only hope was to take desperate measures. He surfaced, and then ran at full speed through the night. Shells exploded just astern. The destroyers drew closer, gaining ground with each passing minute. Providentially, a fleet of native fishing boats suddenly loomed ahead in the dark. The Spyron submarine glided among the small craft, and in the confusion that followed, managed to break contact with the enemy.

At another time, Parsons left his submarine in a rubber boat to reach some local guerrillas. He rowed across a dark harbor, and climbed aboard what he took to be a friendly *batel,* one of the graceful Filipino sailboats frequently seen along the coast. Everyone on deck seemed to be asleep except for the guard—who challenged him in Japanese.

For a moment, Parsons was too stunned to move. As he regained his wits and raced back to the rail to hurl himself overboard, the rest of the enemy soldiers awoke. One of them thrust out a knife, cutting Parsons' jaw open.

With blood pouring from the wound, and bullets peppering the water around him, he managed to swim ashore. Luckily, the guerrillas were near at hand. They brought him to a native doctor who was able to close the deep gash with a bandage, until he could return to the sub for proper stitching.

Month by month, without letup, the work of Spyron went on. New intelligence stations were established at strategic points along the coasts. They were manned by specially trained Filipino and American operators who were carried to their isolated posts on Spyron submarines.

Parsons continued to move among the islands, a half-dozen varied projects always in need of attention. He maintained contact with Colonel Kangleon on Leyte, and with Colonel Fertig and his commanders on Mindanao. He finally met Major Peralta on Panay, and brought his aggressive army of twelve thousand guerrillas into the Spyron network. He left Charley Smith on Samar, and eventually the captain gained control of the difficult situation there. By then, Negros, Bohol, and Cebu had been organized as well, leaving Luzon as the only major island without a large-scale guerrilla movement.

The enemy was too strong on Luzon to permit a show of open defiance. But there were other possibilities, and Parsons soon established an espionage network, with some of its members operating inside Manila.

During one of his later visits to Mindanao, Parsons met his old friend Senator Ozamis at a secret guerrilla hideout. By then the senator had joined the Luzon spy operation, and when he came south to meet Parsons, he brought valuable information with him.

After he had heard the senator's report, Parsons asked him a final question. "Do you have any news of Mrs. Blanche Jurika, Katsy and Tommy's mother?"

The senator grew still. "I was afraid you might ask me that," he said at last. "And even if you hadn't, I would have told you. When a certain plan misfired—because a traitor, as you know, was able to reveal part of it to the Japanese— many people in Manila were arrested. Mrs. Jurika was one of them. She has been sentenced to thirty-five years in prison."

"But she didn't have any connection with the spy ring."

"No, she didn't. But she does have a connection with Commander Parsons, who is very much wanted by the Japanese. The price for your capture keeps rising. The other day, I read that the Japanese Government considers you worth $50,000, dead or alive."

The senator paused. Then he added: "You can do nothing for Mrs. Jurika directly, Chico. It would be fatal, if you tried. But at least for the time being she is in good hands. Her guards are loyal Filipinos, and they'll know what steps to take if the Japanese show signs of molesting her. In the meantime, we are doing everything we can to protect her, and to make other arrangements for her future safety. . . ."

They stood up and shook hands, and later that day, they parted. Parsons did not see his friend again. There was another traitor in Manila, and a few weeks after their meeting, the name of Senator Ozamis was whispered to the Kempeitai.

After they had delivered their cargoes among the islands, Spyron submarines made it a practice to take on passengers for the return trip to Australia. For a few months, while space was limited, only those who were of political or military importance could be evacuated. But the addition of two spacious cargo-carrying submarines meant that a more flexible policy could be inaugurated; soon, a campaign was under way to get in touch with American civilians, and to bring out as many of the refugees as possible.

Scores of such hapless men and women were still living in the central and southern islands. For more than a year they had refused to surrender, preferring a hand-to-mouth existence in the backcountry to life in a civilian prison camp. Initially, the Japanese had made little effort to round them up, but gradually the enemy's attitude had hardened.

At the beginning of 1944, the occupation authorities issued a new edict. It read: "The amnesty under which Americans have been guaranteed safety and internment by the Imperial Japanese Government is about to expire. After 25 January, any American found in the Islands, whether unsurrendered soldier or civilian, will be executed without trial."

After that, the rescue operation became a matter of even greater urgency. The necessity for haste was emphasized by the radio message that Colonel Fertig's guerrillas received on Mindanao, before the January 25th deadline. It came from Major Peralta: "Report thirteen American nationals, among them women and children, have just been slaughtered on Panay." Clearly the Japanese had begun a reign of terror, and Parsons was granted permission by Southwest Pacific Headquarters to increase his efforts to save as many lives as possible.

The Spyron fleet took many additional risks to bring out the refugees. A submarine is never more vulnerable than when it has surfaced or is lying immobile in shallow water. Time and again Spyron subs had to linger for several days just offshore. Often the rendezvous had to be changed before the refugees could be led down by local guerrillas from hiding places in the hills.

The last hours were always the most perilous. After the submarine rose, small native boats carried the civilians, a few at a time, across the shallows. At any moment an enemy patrol boat might suddenly arrive and begin firing. But the submarine waited patiently while the native boats sailed back and forth from shore. Only when the last passengers were aboard did the anxious crew take the sub down again to safety.

Inside, the civilians quietly accepted their new situation. Quarters were extremely cramped. The refugees lived in the forward and after torpedo rooms, which they shared with the chief torpedoman and his crew. There was no privacy. Sailors and passengers slept in their clothes. A few cots were set out for the old and sick, but most of the refugees spent the night curled up in blankets on the steel plates of the decks.

If General Quarters was sounded and the submarine

went into action, the passengers maintained at least an outward calm. They stayed in their assigned places, and tried to keep out of the crew's way. Among the children there was never any anxiety. Occasionally a submarine came under enemy attack, but the youngsters always seemed to assume that the exploding depth charges were really their own ship's deck guns, firing at the enemy, and no one aboard saw the point of disclosing the truth.

Morale rose in the Spyron fleet, thanks to the refugees. The sailors shared their cigarettes and clothing with the men, and tried to make the women as comfortable as possible. Many of the passengers were underweight, and the crews did all they could to feed them up while they were aboard.

The refugee children were the particular favorites of the sailors. Between duty watches, Spyron crewmen cut and sewed together spruce outfits for their smallest passengers, and when the ships made port, the children marched off in well-turned-out naval uniforms.

In all, because of the courage of Spyron's officers and men, more than 450 American civilians were spirited out of the enemy-held Islands. For most of them, the voyage to Australia meant an escape from almost certain death. Few of his organization's achievements gave Parsons more satisfaction than the success of the Spyron submarines in rescuing the innocent people who had been stranded in the Philippines.

Saving civilian lives was only one of the many Spyron activities that enraged the Japanese, and that made Commander Charles Parsons the most-wanted man from Zamboanga all the way north to Tokyo. In August, 1944, enemy newspapers and radios proclaimed triumphantly that a group of guerrillas had been executed, among them "the notorious Charles Parsons."

The item was picked up and widely reported in the United States. Less than a week later, Katsy Parsons received a telegram in North Carolina:

PAY NO ATTENTION TO JAPANESE WISHFUL THINKING. THE REWARD FOR PARSONS IS STILL UNCLAIMED.

The wire was signed CHICK.

15

SPYRON
FLOURISHES

IN OCTOBER, 1944, ALMOST THREE YEARS AFTER THE
fall of Manila, American forces were finally ready to return
to the Philippine Islands. By then, Spyron had completed
the main part of its mission. Every guerrilla in the southern
and central islands was armed with a modern rifle, carbine,
or automatic weapon. Thousands of rounds of ammunition
had been stockpiled in the hills. A hundred coast-watcher
stations were in operation, providing intelligence to American commanders in all branches of the service. A network
of guerrilla radio transmitters was on the alert, awaiting the
signal to begin sending and receiving vital messages in support of the invasion.

Less than two weeks before D-day, Parsons was summoned to General Walter Krueger's headquarters in Hollandia, New Guinea. At a staff meeting there, he was told that Mindanao, the southernmost island, would not be the invasion target, as everyone had supposed. Instead, after a preliminary four-day bombardment, the United States Sixth Army, escorted by a huge armada of submarines, surface ships, and aircraft carriers, would land along the eastern coast of Leyte.

It was evident to those attending the staff meeting in Hollandia that some way would have to be found to coordinate the entire guerrilla effort; it was equally clear that the Underground forces in the central and southern islands would have to be alerted, even before the start of the preliminary bombardment.

Once the actual landings had begun, the guerrillas would be called upon to perform a variety of tasks. On Leyte itself, Colonel Kangleon's soldiers would operate in close support of the main American forces; on Samar, the guerrillas under Captain Charles Smith would assist American diversionary landings; on Mindanao, where the enemy only recently had brought in large troop reinforcements, big coastal guns, and several squadrons of planes, the 30,000-man guerrilla army of Colonel Fertig would harass the enemy, limiting any attempts that might be made to reinforce garrisons to the north.

The native population on Leyte presented a special problem. General MacArthur was extremely anxious to avoid civilian casualties. Somehow, loyal Filipinos had to be removed from target areas without revealing any military information to the enemy. Radio communication with

Colonel Kangleon was out of the question. Messages could be intercepted too easily. An agent would have to see the guerrilla leader in person, an agent who would carry in his head the entire plans for the invasion. After a short time, General Krueger and his staff reluctantly agreed with Parsons: He was the best man available for the assignment.

His return to Leyte had to be made with the utmost secrecy. This time, Parsons decided against using a submarine. Surigao Strait would have to be crossed; it was heavily mined, and there was no possibility of clearing a channel through the minefields without attracting considerable attention. In addition, the best landing point for a submarine was on the wrong side of the island—some eight or ten days' march from Colonel Kangleon's present headquarters. By the time he could reach the guerrilla chief, the American armada would be far at sea, and the preinvasion bombardment would have begun.

The only way to return quickly enough to Leyte would be on a navy flying boat. The Catalinas were slow, cumbersome planes, and offered an easy target for enemy fighters. But there was no alternative. At 8:00 P.M., on October 11th, Parsons, accompanied by an Army Intelligence officer, Colonel Rawolle, climbed aboard a flying boat and stowed away his maps, codes, and other gear. Their pilot raced the motors, and the Catalina took off for Leyte.

The flight plan allowed them four hours to reach one of three alternative sites. If all went well, they would land unobserved at midnight, and establish contact with friendly natives before morning.

But they soon discovered that violent storms covered the entire area and that no landing was possible. Disconsolately, Parsons and the navy pilot agreed to turn south, and at dawn they were back at the base, with fuel tanks almost empty.

Time was becoming extremely critical. Early the same afternoon, a fresh crew came aboard the plane. Daylight made the flight even more hazardous, and the pilot took unusual measures to escape detection. He held the Catalina just six or eight feet above the water during the entire trip, and followed a roundabout course to the east of the islands, in order to clear radar stations and visual observers. After several hours, he swung into a half-circle and raced north, between tiny Dinagat and Homonhon islands, toward the landing site.

As the Catalina touched down, there was a heavy jar and then another, and finally the crashing sound of water sweeping under the pontoons. While the plane taxied, Parsons and his companion pitched their rubber boat into the water, flung in their gear, and dived into the boat themselves. The Catalina gunned her motors, and roared away. She was a speck in the distance when Parsons glanced at his watch. The entire maneuver had taken only sixty seconds.

Good fortune favored them after that. They reached shore without meeting the enemy, and slept most of the night on the floor of a native hut. The next morning guerrilla soldiers arrived in the village to investigate reports of a plane seen landing in the vicinity. Parsons and the colonel identified themselves. Soon they were aboard a motor launch that carried them along the coast as far as a jungle trail leading to one of Colonel Kangleon's radio stations. By the evening of October 13th, a little more than forty-eight hours before the start of the preinvasion bombardment, Parsons was able to send a message to Southwest Pacific Headquarters: *Party arrived safely.*

The next day, Parsons traveled a few miles inland to guerrilla headquarters. When they met in the jungle, he told Colonel Kangleon that on the sixteenth, American aircraft would begin to strike Japanese strongpoints in the central and southern islands. Therefore, it was essential that all civilians be removed at once from the target areas. The colonel assured him that the necessary steps to accomplish this would be taken on Leyte. Parsons' orders did not permit him to reveal the fact that a full-scale invasion would soon be launched, but he felt sure that the colonel, an experienced soldier, understood what was taking place.

Parsons then explained that the bombings would continue intermittently for several days. Because of this, the people would have to remain in the hills until it was safe for them to return to their homes. It would be up to the various guerrilla leaders to see that they did so.

Finally, American Headquarters assumed that the heavy bombardments would drive many of the enemy soldiers out of garrison and field positions. Colonel Kangleon promised to have his guerrilla squads stationed along every road and trail so that the retreating Japanese would find themselves surrounded, with no path of escape.

During October 14th and 15th, hundreds of military

reports poured into Colonel Kangleon's headquarters from guerrilla agents on Cebu, Samar, Mindanao, and Leyte, and Parsons was able to encode and transmit the information to the American forces. Late on the fifteenth, a different sort of report was received. It concerned Tacloban, the capital of Leyte. By now, the American fleet had been observed at sea, and the Japanese realized that an invasion of the Islands was imminent. Tacloban was one of the most likely bombing targets. Without prior warning, the Japanese commander on Leyte had just ordered all but two hundred of his soldiers to withdraw from the city. Every exit was sealed, and the townspeople were being prevented from leaving. When the bombs fell, there would be a civilian massacre. Later, the Japanese would be able to shout "Atrocity!" to the world, and perhaps shatter much of the Islanders' faith in America's good intentions.

Parsons knew that in less than a week a large landing force was scheduled to come ashore on the beach below the capital and that the bombardment of the city would be particularly heavy. Hurrying to his radio he sent out a frantic message to the air force and the navy: *Spare Tacloban. There are only civilians in the city.*

Colonel Kangleon had an additional reason for being concerned about the fate of the capital. His two children, as well as his sister and brother-in-law, were being held prisoner there. Parsons suggested sending in agents to attempt a last-minute rescue, but the colonel stubbornly refused. If the attempt were successful, he pointed out, it would only result in retaliations against other captives. "My youngsters," the guerrilla leader said, "will have to take their chances with everyone else." He spoke with a statesman's sense of duty, but underneath he endured a father's agony.

That night, there was no way of telling whether or not the last-minute message had been received by American forces. The next morning, B-24 bombers appeared over the city and made their first raids. They struck Japanese beach defenses and gun emplacements, right up to the walls of the houses. In all, the bombings lasted four days, but not a single bomb fell on the capital during the raids.

On the twentieth, the huge guns of the fleet blasted the beaches below Tacloban, pulverizing the few concrete pill-boxes and gun emplacements the bombers had missed. They came close to the town, but no shells struck inside the walls.

All morning long, on the twentieth, the assault forces swarmed ashore below the capital, as they did at other landing sites on Leyte. The city fell, and before long, Colonel Kangleon learned that his children, and the other members of his family, were unharmed. Their lives, and the lives of thousands of others in Tacloban, had been saved by the colonel's own guerrilla agents and by a single message sent over a Spyron radio.

When the beachheads had been secured, General MacArthur and his staff came ashore. The campaign to liberate the Islands was far from over, but America's promise to her faithful ally was being redeemed.

"I shall return," the general had said, almost thirty months ago. Now, as he stood on the shore of Leyte, the people of the Philippines knew that he had kept his pledge.

16

THE END
OF THE STORY

STEP BY INEVITABLE STEP, THE SECOND WORLD WAR DREW
to a close. On the far side of the world, Russian and Allied armies overran Nazi Germany, met at the river Elbe,
and in May, 1945, accepted the surrender of the German
Government. In the Pacific, vast battles were waged on sea,
on land, and in the air. The liberation of the Philippines
required much bitter fighting, while Iwo Jima and then
Okinawa became the sites of still more bloodshed. At last,
with America's Pacific forces poised to invade the home
islands of Japan, the destruction of Hiroshima and Naga-
saki by atomic bombs forced Japanese bitter-end militarists
from power, enabling moderate leaders to sue for peace. By
then, almost six years had passed since the outbreak of the
worldwide conflict.

Following the landings on Leyte, Chick Parsons suffered a recurrence of malaria, and returned to the United States on leave. He had not seen Katsy or their three boys in more than a year and a half. He remained briefly in North Carolina, and then, in January, 1945, returned to duty in the Philippines. Until enemy resistance ended in the Islands, he continued to work with local guerrilla forces, and when Manila fell to American soldiers on February 3rd, he entered the city close behind them.

Not long afterward, he wrote: "Manila is . . . completely demolished. I have seen sights that I shall remember a long time. I arrived on the heels of the Yanks as they pushed the enemy down the Boulevard toward the Luneta, and visited the house of a good friend. . . . In the garden of the house I counted twenty-two bodies—the entire family, including women and children, three people who were visiting at the time, and servants—liquidated in a most brutal fashion. . . . A number of my other friends have suffered a like fate."

He did not find Katsy's mother, Blanche Jurika, among those released from the Manila civilian prison. He wrote to a friend: "Katsy's mother had been taken from Welfareville with four other women just before the invasion of Manila. She was not at Santiago or Muntinglupa. There is a faint chance that she may be at Baguio, which is still [enemy] held—but I am afraid she has paid heavily for being my mother-in-law. So far Tommy Jurika, her son—who is on duty here with me—and I have both drawn a blank."

Peace finally came to the Islands—and then, Independence. The first President of the Philippine Republic, Sergio Osmeña, took up his duties in Malacanan Palace. The capital began to revive, and many peacetime residents, like Chick and Katsy Parsons and their three sons, returned to their former homes.

By the war's end, Parsons had become one of America's most decorated heroes. His awards included the Navy Cross; a Gold Star in lieu of a second Navy Cross; the Army Distinguished Service Cross; the Bronze Star Medal; the Asiatic-Pacific Campaign Medal; the Philippine Defense Ribbon with one bronze star; the Philippine Liberation Ribbon with two bronze stars; the Naval Reserve Medal; and the Army Distinguished Unit Badge with Oak Leaf Cluster. He also had been awarded the Distinguished Service Star by President Manuel Quezon of the Philippines, and the Medal for Valor—the Philippines' equivalent of America's highest military award, the Congressional Medal of Honor.

Only nine men have ever received the Medal for Valor. Four were Americans: General MacArthur, Admiral Chester Nimitz, General Jonathan Wainwright, and Commander Charles Parsons.

The war that Chick Parsons had fought was a silent, unconventional one. His troops were ragged, often very young men, equipped with old, makeshift weapons. But the Filipino guerrillas had been armed with something more— an unquenchable thirst for freedom. Many of them deserved decorations for valor, but there was no one to bestow such awards.

Thousands of ordinary Filipino civilians matched the guerrillas in courage. They sheltered their country's soldiers, fed them, and concealed their whereabouts when interrogated by the enemy—civilians who sometimes gave their lives as a result. For most of them, there were no awards, either.

It was the fortunate Filipino or American family in the Islands that had not suffered its losses. The Parsons family was no exception. Shortly after peace returned, an American soldier, Master Sergeant Richard Sakakida, testified to a wartime experience. While a prisoner of war in the Philippines, he had been required to serve as an interpreter for the Japanese Army. His affidavit said:

"Prior to the month of August, 1944, a group of persons, approximately 80 in number, had been tried by Courts-Martial and convicted of guerrilla activities with the Filipino and American guerrilla forces. Of the total tried, certain persons, between 18 and 40 in number, were sentenced to be executed. On or about the 25th of August, 1944, those so sentenced were executed by decapitation in what is known as the Chinese Cemetery, north of the city of Manila. These executions were under the supervision of . . . a civilian with rank equivalent to a lieutenant in the army, [who was] then serving as Prison Warden at Old Bilibid Prison in Manila.

"I was required to witness the above executions.

"I distinctly recall that among those executed was one Mrs. Blanche W. Jurika."

Twenty people were executed. A mausoleum was built in

the cemetery, to honor their common grave. It keeps alive the memory of those who died for freedom in the Islands, American and Filipino, soldier and civilian—a small monument to remind later generations of the bitter struggle of an earlier day.

INDEX

American forces, return of, to the Islands, 145-151

Australia
Gen. MacArthur ordered to, 45
Philippine Government-in-Exile in, 45

Bataan, 22, 28, 29, 30, 40, 44, 71
Death March from, 46, 118
MacArthur's stand at, 29
retreat to, 39
surrender of, 46
Bowler (guerrilla), 86, 87, 100

Cavite Naval Base, 18, 22, 23
destruction of, 30, 31
Cebu, 55, 111, 150
civilian casualties, measures taken to avoid, 30, 146-151
civilian exchange, 53, 54
Clark Field, Japanese attack on, 27
"Co-Prosperity Sphere," 42
Corregidor, 28, 30, 31, 40, 44, 71
fortress of, 18, 46
MacArthur at, 29
surrender of, 52, 53, 72, 118

Doolittle, Col. James, Tokyo raided by, 50

Dyess, Col. Wm., 118, 119, 125, 128

Europe, war in, 18-20
evacuees, 56-64
Evans, Col., 65-70
executions in Manila, 155-156

Fertig, Col. Wendell, 78, 79, 85-87, 89, 100, 101, 102, 105, 111, 115-116, 118, 131, 136, 139, 141, 146
Fort Santiago, Parsons imprisoned at, 48-50, 51

guerrillas, Filipino, 68, 69, 76, 78, 79, 83, 85, 87, 90-93, 94, 106-109
beginning of, 74
courage of, 154-155
leadership for, 74, 100
MacArthur approval of, 70, 75, 97
organization of, 96
Parsons dossier on, 113-114, 118
role of, during American invasion, 146
supplies for, 72, 77, 84, 85, 98-99
weapons for the, 145
See also Fertig; Spyron

Hawaii, Japanese attack on, 23-24

Hedges (guerrilla), 86, 87, 111
See also Mindanao

Homma, Gen., 32
arrival of, in Manila, 34

Hull, Cordell, 21

independence
Filipino desire for, 16
U.S. promise of, for Philippines, 42, 45

intelligence file, the Parsons', 41, 52, 53, 54, 57-58, 59-62, 65

Japan
embargo against, 20, 21
Filipino hatred of, 42, 46
invasion of, 152
peace talks between U.S. and, 21
United States relations with, 19

Jurika, Blanche, 17, 25, 32, 35, 36, 43, 51, 53, 55, 84, 117
execution of, 155
imprisonment of, 140, 153

Jurika, Katrushka (Katsy), 17
See also Parsons, Katsy

Jurika, Stephen, 17

Jurika, Tommy, 17, 55, 85, 117, 153
a member of Spyron, 118

Kangleon, Col. Ruperto, 97-100, 111, 136, 139, 146, 147
family of, 149-151
See also Leyte

Kempeitai (Japanese secret police), 40, 54, 58, 63, 137

Kincaid, Admiral, 99

Krueger, Gen. Walter, 146, 147

Leyte, 69, 71, 92, 94, 111, 136, 139, 146, 147, 150, 151, 153
guerrillas on, 96-100
See also Kangleon

Luzon, 14, 52, 71, 112
destruction of American planes on, 27-28
Japanese invasion of, 29
organized resistance on, 46
Parsons family on, 17
unorganized resistance on, 42-44, 68
See also Manila

Luzon Stevedoring Company, 18
a part of U.S. Navy, 24

MacArthur, Gen. Douglas, 22, 29, 70, 71, 73, 75, 76, 78, 79, 83, 86, 88, 97, 99, 100, 101, 102, 105, 110, 113, 116, 136, 146
arrival of, at Corregidor, 29
in Australia, 68
departure of, from the Philippines, 45
guerrilla organization approved by, 70, 75
Medal of Valor awarded to, 154

promise made by, 45, 136, 137

return of, to the Islands, 151

MacLish, Lt. Col. Ernest, 86, 87, 90, 93, 97

McCarthy, Capt., 131-133

McCoy, Commander Melvin, 118, 126, 129, 130, 133

Manila, 112
  Americans return to, 153
  bombing of, 27-28
  crisis in, 20-21, 22, 24
  demolition work in, 30-31, 38
  fall of, 27-38, 39
  Japanese in possession of, 35
  an open city, 30, 31
  the Parsons in, 14, 15, 17-18, 20
  See also Luzon

Manila Telephone Company, Parsons' job with, 15

Medal for Valor, recipients of the, 154

Medina, Capt., 130

Melnick, Col. Stephen, 118

Meyer-Muzzall & Company, Parsons' job with, 15

Mindanao, 16, 17, 69, 71, 78, 79, 86-90, 105, 111, 115, 139, 140, 146, 150
  Commander Parsons' return to, 80-83
  Parsons' familiarity with, 16
  Tenth Military District of, 88
  See also, Fertig; Hedges; Pendatun

Narra Maru, captured Japanese ship used by Parsons, 89-95

Nimitz, Adm. Chester, 154

Osmena, Sergio, 30, 154

Ozamis, Senator, 110-111, 112, 113, 140-141

Pacific Fleet, American, damage to, at Pearl Harbor, 39

Panay, 68, 111
  Americans killed on, 142
  See also Peralta

Parsons, Charles (Chick)
  arrest of, 43, 47
  arrival of, in Philippines, 11-14
  awards won by, 154
  background of, 12, 14-15
  children of, 17, 25, 32, 36, 40, 43, 51, 59-60, 61-63, 64, 85
  as Consul of Panama, 28-29, 36-38
  diplomatic passport for, 29, 36
  imprisonment of, at Fort Santiago, 48-50, 51
  jobs held by, in the Philippines, 14-16
  jungle flight of, 118-134
  as lt. commander, 64, 65, 75
  marriage of, 17
  Naval Reserve duty of, 16, 23-24
  reward for capture of, 14, 144
  wartime duty of, as Navy lieutenant, 24, 28-33

Parsons, Charles (*continued*)
  See also "Spyron"
Parsons family, evacuation of, 56-64
Parsons, Katsy, 24, 31-37, 40, 41, 43, 47-55, 57, 59, 62, 63, 64, 65, 85, 144
Pearl Harbor, 23
  American Pacific Fleet damaged at, 39
  bombing of, by Japanese, 24
Pendatun, Salipada, 87, 88, 100-105, 111, 135
  See also Mindanao
Peralta, Macario, 67, 68, 69, 111, 139, 142
  See also Panay
Philippine Government-in-Exile, 45
Philippines
  crisis in, 20, 21, 22
  freedom for, 16, 42
  Japanese occupation of, 73
  liberation of, 152
Portz, Commander, 24

Quezon, Manuel, 30

radio broadcasts, civilian morale maintained by, 136-137
radio programs, special for the Philippines, 136-137
Rawolle, Col., 147
refugees, American, 141-143
Roosevelt, President, 21, 24, 44

Sakakida, Sgt. Richard, 155
Samar, 69, 71, 111, 139, 150

Santo Domingo, Church of, destroyed, 31
Santo Tomás, 57
  internment camp at, 35
  Parsons imprisoned at, 50-51, 53-54
Sayre, Francis, 29
Sharp, Gen. Wm. F., 71, 72
Smith, Capt. Charles, 78, 80, 85, 88, 116, 118, 122-124, 129, 130, 133, 134, 139, 146
Southwest Pacific Theater, 71, 149
"Spyron", 75, 77, 89, 90, 91, 99, 102, 104, 145
  coast-watcher stations for, 110
  submarines assigned to, 135-136, 138, 139, 141, 142
  supplies from, 111-112
submarine rendezvous, 131-134

Tokyo, attack on, by American planes, 50

United States
  neutrality of (1939), 20
  peace talks between Japan and, 21

Valor, recipients of Medal for, 154

Wainwright, Gen. Jonathan, 154
war in Europe, 18-20
  end of, 152
Wood, Gen. Leonard, 14
Wood-Forbes Investigating Commission, 14